Dedicated to and in Memory of my beloved husband

Robin Julian Laflamme (1953-2020)

Gratitude

Special thanks to Guivdo Trepsa, director of the Nicholas Roerich Museum,

for permission to use The Mother of the World painting by Nicholas Roerich on the cover.

319 West 107th Street, New York, NY 10025

To all my students around the world who participated in the Divine Feminine Study Classes at the Sufi Universal Fraternal Institute, https://sufiuniversalfraternalinstitute.live, and for the ongoing development of this text, I give my thanks for their generous contribution and insight. To my beloved husband, Robin whose presence and support made this project an inestimable joy.

Gratitude to Terri Hinte for her expert eye.

Contents

CHAPTER I

CHAPTER II

Foreword

Hidden in Holy Women's intuitive actions are the seeds for spiritual potential that will open a direction to understanding Fourth Wave Feminine Principles. Women who are spiritually motivated and socially responsive in their service to humanity draw us closer to ourselves because their insights and actions have laid clear tracks about how we might understand our own experiences found through compassion resulting in selfless service. The Holy Women whom you will read about in this book are archetype forerunners of our human potential. How they faced the circumstances of their experiences while here on this earth offers us a window into choices sometimes unknown to us as we move through our many stages of evolution. As their experiences and my experiences leap together and consilience is confirmed, a theophanic or unity of the Divine Being shows connection to the mystical source of Oneness, and Fourth Wave Feminine Principles are activated. Doubt vanishes, and one can sense, through the subtle awareness and deep knowing, the Divine connection with Source, the Holy Mother of the World-Gaia.

In this book, I present the stories of Eight Holy Women from many religious belief systems and show how their lives modeled five examination techniques such as transcendental phenomenology, hermeneutics, Sufi esoteric principles, and sociological considerations to bring forward Fourth Wave Feminine awareness, not as a methodology but as a combined progression for illuminating my own experiences as I align with theirs. As a Sufi and transpersonal, postmodern mystic, I therefore include my own experiences as a source of collaborative information and I become the ninth woman in the text. I hope this kind of association will offer insight within the reader's somatic sensing as an example of how one can reveal a natural integration of body/mind/soul through Fourth Wave Feminine Principles that regard other and self as one. Fourth Wave Feminine Principles will teach us how to read ourselves as we are reading others. With the guiding principles of participatory synchronicity, pairing, consilience, and correlation found in "our lived experiences," one can activate the celestial climate that reveals the ever-living teacher, the great Holy Mother of the World-Gaia, who abides in all beings at all times.

(Madona Labores, painting by Nicholas Roerich)

A Prayer to the Divine Mother

Oh Divine Bringer of the People, You reign in the worlds above and below.

You who manifest the stellar life through the many forms of Divine Light and through the many

who have come in the past, are present now, and shall be in the future.

We bow in praise and honor all Your forms.

Your compassion is endless and inexhaustible.

We pray for ever-lasting energy, courage, and wisdom.

May we fulfill Your mighty task of complete surrender to the Divine Creation and shatter every

obstacle with love.

When our hearts yearn to unite, it is Your attraction,

When our eyes shine, it is Your cosmic vastness,

When our souls breathe, it is Your Divine law,

When our bodies die, it is Your ever-lasting presence that remains.

Oh, Powerful Cosmic-walker, shower us with eternal starlight that we may know our Divine origin in You.

Purify us and set us free from the conditioned wheel of forgetfulness.

Make us your lucid instruments of peace and harmony, protectors of the Sacred Feminine and of the innocence of the world.

Brighten our indwelling Shekinah, Chisti, and Ruh.

Cast forth Your uniting web of beneficence within the depths of the earth and into the infinite galaxies.

Sweet Reign

Fourth Wave Feminine Principles

(Mother of the World, Painting by Nicholas Roerich)

by Ana Perez Chisti

Introduction and Purpose

As I contemplated multiple women's hagiographies and how their spiritual understanding turned into awakened awareness, these Holy Women's experiences show how they embodied spiritual gnosis, blending their female and male archetypes while opening a pathway to a Self-reflective reality that mirrored the Holy Mother of the World-Gaia. Their spiritual experiences arose in multiple ways, either through tragedy, cultural pressure, or from following in the footsteps of great prophets such as Jesus, Mohammed, Eagle Spirit, or from one's own mother/father, but most importantly their contribution to the world came from their intuitive development.

As you read into the lives of these Holy Women who are dedicated to a life of devoted service to others, observe what moves you in your arising bodily and emotional senses. Our multiple sense systems have much to offer us. They unite us in a common investigation of what is true about our reasons for being human. They offer a natural epistemological investigation into the way we can discover our journey in the physical form, our intuition, our essence, and our spiritual purpose. This compiled writing is therefore presented through eight women's historical perspectives as they opened their lives to become representatives of the Great World Mother-Gaia. These stories are correlated to my own experiences, which forms nine women in total.

I view myself as a transcendental postmodern mystic who investigates body-mind dualistic attitudes that have caused much confusion in women's lives, particularly about one's essence of being. I respect the physical instrument as a sound source of knowledge and recognize the human body and emotions as a teleological constituent or natural purpose leading all material phenomena into spirit. I unite body and mind, female and male into the phenomena of integral awareness and for evolving a quick, acute, and intuitive understanding of the soul.

For the academic reader, I am using methodologies such as transcendental phenomenology because it provides an accommodating series of patterns that bring correlation to my own experiences as part of a transformative Fourth Wave Feminine Principle. Transcendental Phenomenology brings the personal experience of the Holy Women in a mystical and sacred manner and constellates the awakening of my own self-development that is potentially already here and present. All experiences, whether they are those of the Holy Women or mine, are already schematized to bring to light their spiritual revelations into self-observation. Their selfless actions and their dedicated lives gave rise to my own correlative insights.

I valued hermeneutical approaches because they offer concepts of bridging distance found in textual style, such as women who lived in another century, e.g., Julian of Norwich and Hazrat Babajan, while I gazed upon my own experiences in the modern era.

Hermeneutics as a methodological process and art of interpretation reveals a mysterious intimacy that grips our entire being, where one can find no distance at all between the person we are reading about and the reader. Every encounter with a Holy Women's contribution (even when literarily assessed) brings us closer to "essence," as if there existed a verbal encounter with oneself.

When we regard the effect of language on our somatic understanding, it is necessary to regard an element of proximity, as words can become distinct fragments of the mind that often reach back to earlier periods in our soul's journey where we intuitively sense familiar ground. Hans-Georg Gadamer, a student of Martin Heidegger, details the pathway of remembrance by how the art of speaking and writing also belonged to the earliest Greek philosophical period of Plato and Aristotle, who when saying something esoterically complex sought out a deeper sense of meaning instead of remaining simplistic. How these Holy Women speak directly to us verifies this statement. Similarly, hermeneutics flowered in the Romantic period as a consequence of the modern dissolution of firm bonds of tradition by a theory of knowledge [i] that teaches us how to listen intently to what is being communicated in order to gain insight, or become aware of, a message hidden under the surface. Under this "surface" may be an ancient historic awareness that arises and lives in our intuitive sensing in the moment.

As Frederich Ast said, *"To find the spirit of the whole through the individual, and through the whole then grasp the individual."* [ii] If texts are properly understood, texts of human activity are not as innocuous as they may seem to be, meaning they might not appear during a quick read-through to apply to our present circumstances, but rather there may be reflections of hidden drives, class interests and higher prophetic ideals stimulated in us which is transmitted through their religious and philosophical development. These are ideas found in the preserving elements that still run deeply in hermeneutics. The hermeneutic principle found in multiple religious scriptures offers sharp contrast to sociological fixations because intensified reflection is a basic means of emancipation from authority and tradition. [iii] Thus, Gadamer's idea is very important when we absorb the hagiographies of Julian of Norwich, Mother Teresa, and Mary Baker Eddy, for example.

The Eight Holy Women reflected in this text were chosen for multiple reasons. They represent distinctive spiritual paths of which they were committed practitioners. Mother Teresa of Calcutta, Julian of Norwich, and Mary Baker Eddy represent the Christian religion. They are powerful contributors to social change and to the reconfiguration of women's role in society, most particularly within a religious framework. For example, Mother Teresa served the very poor and disadvantaged of the Hindu population with no assistance forthcoming from the patriarchal-designed organization of the Catholic Church. Although her training was through the Catholic doctrine, she stepped forward into her sacred service as a unique operative and was honored with a Nobel Peace Prize. Mary Baker Eddy served thousands of people from different faith systems that came from a wide range of constituencies. She founded a new religious order, the Christian Science Church, positioning herself as the Prophetic figure in spiritual leadership, denied to women for centuries. She was a healer and activist and although she was not a self-proclaimed feminist, she brought women to a new station of spiritual authority. Julian of Norwich reached into inner visionary depths that inspired large segments of people in the Christian worldview who held male-dominated ascendancy with only male prophetic archetypes within the medieval period. Her visions of seeing Jesus as "Mother" opened new insight into how one experiences the Master Jesus as feminine.

Noor-un-nisa Inayat Khan and Hazrat Babajan represent the Sufi Path and they elicited mastery with mystical levels of willing self-sacrifice and an itinerate lifestyle under the stress of difficult and different sociological situations. Their personality structures were markedly distinct from one another. Noor-un-nisa, the eldest daughter of the famous 19th century Sufi Mystic Hazrat Inayat Khan, was an attractive, gentle, otherworldly woman. Yet, showing courageous warriorship, she served in the armed forces during World War II and worked in the underground French spy network, a position few women ever dreamed of participating in, for the purpose of helping the French people stand against the oppressive Nazi regime.

Hazrat Babajan was a psychically sensitive, itinerate 18th century Sufi master who lived as a homeless woman under a neem tree in male-dominated Mogul India. By her authentic choices to follow her inner spiritual direction and attain the level of respect and authority of one of the greatest Sufi mystics of her time, she became the spiritual mother of many avatars that brought their message to the world such as Hazrat Inayat Khan, Meher Baba, and others.

The Reverend Amanuensis Frida Waterhouse used the exalted spiritual principles of community ethics found in the Jewish religion and culture that helped her serve others from all walks of life. She lived fully and erotically by exploring her female identity against the sociological norms that stymied and profiled females during the 1940s and 1950s. She nurtured spiritual transformative experiences and prophetic insights that were models for social justice as she struggled for equality, identity from oppressive gender profiling, and sought spiritual freedom. She designed inner tools, called a Three Self Method of Inner Inquiry, for those beings seeking deeper meaning and answers to life's questions. She guided thousands of seekers toward the awakening of their inner intuitive processes.

Sanapia, a Comanche Eagle Doctor, reveals a committed life to the "*puhakut,*" a servant of the people who were white or from other Indigenous clans. She found the pathway that allowed "the Medicine" which channeled through her actions and which alleviates human suffering. She reveals a strict life of ritual behavior that had to align ethically with the great work of the Eagle Spirit. She details the constant fight with the malevolent forces that she battled so that the power transmission of the Medicine can be protected.

Dr. Rina Sircar, a Theravadan Buddhist practitioner and professor of Meditation, applied the Buddha Dharma in all applications of life bringing honor and position to women in the Buddhist community that is essentially male-dominated. Rina studied under the great Forest Dwelling Saint, the Venerable Taungpulu Twaya Kaba-Aye Sayadaw in Burma. She received a special transmission that allowed her to access the inner state of serene tranquility brought through her mastery in meditation practice. As an accomplished scholar in the Pali language, the original language, (Magadhi Prakrit) of Buddha Sakyamuni, she detailed the depth of psychological principles uncovered in the Abhidhamma Pitaka, a seven-volume Pali compendium of moral insight and value.

What unites these selected Holy Women culturally is the sociological marginalization of women during their historic time frame. This is not a new subject for investigation as most women face this condition. However, I was interested to explore the inherent intuitive process that was evident in each of the Holy Women mentioned above, how it affected my intuitive process, and how they found their spiritual breakthrough to serve others and thus activated my own spiritual breakthrough.

Over the course of this research, I found a living presence. The spiritual exegetical material uncovered how these Holy Women sensed hidden connections which instructed them to turn oppressive action to their benefit so that their spiritual and prophetic insights could surface revealing a theophanic (or unity) of manifestation by which the Holy Mother of the World-Gaia lives at the interiority of our beings at all times, thus showing the power of Fourth Wave Feminine Principles and the sovereignty of the spiritual life.

As I lived with these Holy Women's experiences, there arose, through consilience and pairing, two processes which synthesized for me transcendental phenomenology and hermeneutical approaches. These helped supply the model for correlation and synchronicity. I found many arising messages hidden under the surface experiences of these Holy Women. You will see from my experiences the changes I encountered. May you also find what you need in these stories and may Fourth Wave Feminine Principles be the key that unlocks the door to integration and manifestation of love for yourself and all beings but especially for the Holy Mother of the World-Gaia.

Fourth Wave Feminism

I have come to understand Fourth Wave Feminine Principles as a pathway into rebuilding the presence of the Holy Mother of the World-Gaia within the intuitive center of every living woman and man. When this center is reestablished, the initiation and thus the access to the Holy Mother Gaia's Divine Essence is reestablished and Her Holy relationship to Her many embodied selves become one in the world community. When this theophany or unified state is accomplished in the female and male individual, it will become clear how each woman and man will fulfill their spiritual function and the purpose of each life will be empowered. A woman's true spiritual state will bring the dominant paradigm into balance and benefit all communities.

We are a part of the Mother of the World-Gaia's great soul. We are invited here on this planet to evolve and to find Her, and we are here as Her guests. The initiation mysteries that all women and men must eventually pass through comes from the initial acknowledgment that we belong to Her in all Her infinite expanded states of being; even that which is empty of Her Divine Presence has within them Her Sacred Seed. It is within the compassionate embrace of the Holy Mother of the World-Gaia that we can see at any given time what we ourselves can understand about Her knowledge; even when we think we are reading about another woman's life, we are essentially reading about our own reflection of Her Divine life that is part of us and of which we are all composed. When the initiation into the mystery of how the Divine Mother of World-Gaia opens in the consciousness of body, mind, and spirit, the eschatological secrets that reveal Her reality in Divine manifestation are brought to light.

Fourth Wave Feminine Principles are built on clear feminine experiences that guide women and men ever further into intuitive mastery, independence, and interdependence. Fourth Wave Feminine Principles are sacred mystical principles that have guided the initiate from the beginning of creation but have remained hidden. Many biographies are written about the outer facts of Holy Women's lives, such as where the women lived, whom they met, etc. But the inner realities were about their experiences and the secret mystical consciousness that changed their purpose and the lives of all they encountered.

To understand Fourth Wave Feminine development, let us briefly review the three major steps that the early Feminist Movement encountered. There is much literature written on these facts and about those brilliant women who brought advancement to the development of women's condition in society. Restating the history of Feminist development is not the purpose of this text, but I wish to simply review some of the early Feminist Movement issues and the steps that were taken for the purpose of developmental coherence that builds into the Fourth Wave.

The First, Second, and Third Wave Feminist Movement

First Wave Feminist Movement was built on the clear legal direction of women suffrage (the right to vote). It was a title was given in the 1970s, which addressed the legal inequities that kept all women from participating in the political development of the USA. This first movement came to the forefront in the early 19th century America and extended to the United Kingdom. It brought cohesion to the suppression of women in many areas of life where sociological codification of women's roles was strongly upheld, such as not being able to vote and not being able to hold a job or high office in

18

many professions, including any position in spiritual/religious authority by existing religions. Wide-ranging conservative Christian groups led by Frances Willard and the Women's Christian Temperance Union with Matilda Joslyn Gage, who started the National Women's Suffrage Association, were key players for activating women and awakening them to the sociological inequities that held women's freedom under a male-domination strategy. Leaders in First Wave Feminist Movement were Lucretia Coffen Mott, Elizabeth Cady Stanton, Lucy Stone, and Susan B. Anthony, to name a few. Many more gave their effort and their lives, and they are honored in our hearts.

Second Wave Feminist Movement surged in the 1960s and held strong until the 1970s, emphasizing legal obstacles but rather placing attention on other kinds of inequities that kept women marginalized, such as nonequal pay for same kinds of work, and reviewing gender-biased classifications within all job structures. Second Wave Feminists wanted to know why doctors were in the majority men, and nurses were in the majority women. Few colleges were open to co-education, and with the activation of the Second Wave Movement, Mills, Radcliffe, and Smith Colleges became leading edge in that they sponsored women's education instead of male education. Although plans were laid out for Planned Parenthood in Second Wave Feminist Movement, it did not come into full development until Third Wave took flight. Leaders of Second Wave Feminist Movement were Betty Friedan, Simone de Beauvoir, Kate Millett, and Carol Hanisch. There are many more who stepped forward and changed the biased frame of thinking, and we honor and salute their effort.

Third Wave Feminist Movement in the 1990s was a revolution and became a backlash to the failures created in the Second Wave Movement in the 1960s. Women's voices became centered on Planned Parenthood, free choice about who decides how a woman should treat her body when faced with unwanted pregnancies (Roe vs. Wade), and the crisis of having too many children when under duress of severe financial limitation. The big issues that were directly on the table were those that dealt with sexual harassment in the workplace, the glass ceiling in the job market, misogynistic advertisement and use of women's body for marketing products, single motherhood, unfair maternity leave in the workplace, and central issues about how women are racially treated and classified because of their sexuality in a social dominant paradigm that continues to favor men over women. All these issues brought out immense anger and hatred against men, and the movement met many blockages. The women who were well known in this period were Gloria Steinem, Betty Friedan, bell hooks, and Eve Ensler's Vagina Monologues brought disappointments from women's stories into focus. These women require our deep respect as they fought through difficult marginalization, but within the misery of separation and condemnation of the male gender, a thread in humanity was broken that continues to require healing.

In Fourth Wave Feminism Principles, my hope for you as women and men is that your experience of these Eight Holy Women becomes a gateway into yourselves, your intuition, and your spiritual purpose toward a greater harmony. I include my experiences as the ninth woman in this book indicating how the intuitive process is paired through the insights of my life when inspired by other women's authentic experiences that arise through the theophany or unity of being part of the Divine Mother of the World-Gaia acting through them to me. As co-learners, I propose we begin approaching Holy Women's hagiographies in a Fourth Wave Feminine postmodern way. For me, this came about by experimenting with multiple ideas that flow from transcendental approaches, pairing co-presence and consilience. These approaches, later defined in the text, can open vistas into intuitive hidden potential and mystical realities within us while at the same time regarding our body's subtle sensing system and emotion as instruments of balance and knowledge. May the synthesis of awareness also happen for you and may you be truly blessed in your process.

Mother Teresa (1910-1997) – The Independent Missionary

The basic information of Mother Teresa's early life and development can be found in many texts and websites. Facts are synthesized below for a brief overview but the extraction for my meaning of synchronicity was taken from a moment in Mother Teresa's early life cited in Katherine Sprink's biographical account.[iv]

Mother Teresa was born Agnes Gonxha Bojaxhiu on August 26, 1910, and she died on September 5, 1997. Agnes was born in Skopje, which today is a capital of the Republic of Macedonia. She was the youngest of the children of an Albanian family from Shkoder, born to Nikola and Drane Bojaxhiu. Her father was involved in the politics of the day and was devoted to the Albanian Cause. After a political meeting in 1919, he fell ill and died. Agnes at the time was about 8 years old. Her father's death was shocking for the whole family as it caused fear about how the family was going to survive. Women during that period were confined to a social life of wife and mother, and marriages were usually arranged within closed systems of family negotiation. Her mother, seeking protection in her faith, directed Agnes to the Catholic Church. After her father's death, her mother raised her as a Roman Catholic.

According to a biography by Graff Clucas, [v] during her early years Agnes was fascinated by stories of the lives of missionaries and their service. By the time she was 12, she was convinced that she should commit herself to religious life. [vi] She left her home at age 18 to join the Sisters of the Loreto as a missionary.

At that time Loreto Sisters were a branch of the Institute of the Blessed Virgin Mary founded by an Englishwoman, Mary Ward, in 1609. Mary Ward had a vision for a different mode of religious life for women. She envisioned women living a life in companionship and discernment, inspired by the gospel and engaging with the world without the constraints of the traditional cloister, or an established "Rule," placing them under the governance of men. She also believed that women were equal to men in intellect and should be educated accordingly. These principles appealed to Agnes and she set out to join the Loreto Sisters, but she did not realize she would never again set eyes on her mother or sister.[vii]

Agnes initially went to the Loreto Abbey in Rathfarnham, Ireland in order to learn English, which was the language of the Sisters of Loreto. They used English when instructing schoolchildren in India. Arriving in India in 1929, she began her novitiate in Darjeeling, near the Himalayan Mountains. She took her first vows as a nun on May 24, 1931. At that time she chose the name Teresa after the patron saint of missionaries. She took her solemn vows on May 14, 1937, while serving as a teacher at the Loreto convent school in eastern Calcutta. Although Teresa enjoyed teaching at the school, she was increasingly disturbed by the poverty surrounding Calcutta. A famine in 1943 brought misery and death to the city, and the outbreak of Hindu/Muslim violence in August 1946 plunged the city into despair and horror.

Three years later, Teresa experienced what she later described as "the call within the call" while traveling to the Loreto convent in Darjeeling for her annual retreat. *"I was to leave the convent and help the poor while living among them. It was an order; to fail would have been to break the faith."* [viii] It is here that we begin to realize the impact of the intuitional message that would become embodied as an act of social justice on Mother Teresa's future choices. Although she identified herself as a Loreto, she knew this moment would separate her from the Loreto Sisters. She began her missionary work with the poor in 1948, replacing her traditional Loreto habit with a simple white cotton *chira* decorated with a blue border and then venturing out into the slums. [ix] The rest of her work is legendary and fills hundreds of books.

An important element of her "intuitive-sensing" arises in the experience she details below. After her death, a diary was found with a description of the difficulties she faced at the beginning of her time in Calcutta. She had no food, income, or place to stay. She had to resort to begging and loneliness. This experience was a key factor for her feeling sense and awareness of what the poor were feeling and dealing with on a daily basis.

In Kathryn Sprink's (1997) book,[x] she referred to a comment Mother Teresa made about the doubt that rose up in her awareness including the desire to return to the convent:

> *Our Lord wants me to be a free nun covered with the poverty of the cross. Today I learned a good lesson. The poverty of the poor must be so hard for them. While looking for a home I walked and walked till my arms and legs ached. I thought how much they must ache in body and soul, looking for a home, food and health. Then the comfort of the Loreto (her former Order) came to tempt me. "You only*

have to say the word and all is yours again," the Tempter kept saying. Of free

choice, my God, and out of love for you, I desire to remain and do whatever be

your Holy will in my regard. I did not let a single tear come. [xi]

Knowing the plight of the poor, Mother Teresa's inner dialogue with what she
called "the Tempter" illuminates a bridge that brought two areas of knowing together.
An awareness of the temptation for an easier life, protected by the church, counteracted
an altruistic understanding that motivated her actions. The scale of human suffering she
saw around her and knowing she could not tolerate it personally activated the
commitment within to serve and led her into her life's work. Instead of being repelled in
hysteria toward safety and helplessness in a male-dominated religious structure, she
took action toward that which she experienced from suffering. Even though the odds of
receiving help from the Roman Catholic Church headed in the 1960s by Pope John
XXIII brought little hope for change in women's relationship with the Church, during
the second Vatican council the recognition of women began to take on a central theme of
exploration. Women were beginning to be recognized as valuable and were finally seen
as members who could offer something besides monetary resources to the Church.
Mother Teresa had the centers in Calcutta well established by the time the Church
started paying attention to her projects.

Mother Teresa proved how every revelation could become one's religion. Every
mundane experience that integrated her physical form of knowing with her purpose
became her spiritual path. As Mother Teresa moved closer to her inner sensing of what
was right for her core nucleus of being, her actions moved closer to her conscious action,
and with sympathetic resonance, her structure of reality was altered. She felt connected
to humanity because her body remembered the same level of suffering, and her work

moved her closer to the Divine creation: the human being who suffers alone and who is homeless and starving.

When vision and action leap together a new direction is born in the heart of the individual. A person who risks following the bodies sensing intelligence knows without a shadow of doubt how they might risk what it feels like to walk on an unknown path. In Mother Teresa's case, she somatically understood suffering as the same experience as those she served. When she finally realized how untenable the condition of famine and homelessness was, she proceeded to dedicate her life to its prevention.

Consilience

Mother Teresa reveals an archetypal story of rejection and redirection, which I remembered from a particular incident of separation and loneliness in my life. This experience left an indelible cellular memory pattern in my body and, like Mother Teresa, it helped me identify with those that had the same experience. It was not for a long time that I lived in the condition of homelessness and hunger, but it was long enough to frame an inter-subjective apprehension of why I was here on earth again and what it was that I needed to do with the time that I had been given.

Awakening to an expectation of safety by assuming the day would unfold the way I predicted it would was removed. The urgency of an empty stomach, of not knowing where I was going to live, brought up feelings of desperation, loneliness, and shame. Shame of failure in one's eyes can bring a feeling of hysteria and feelings like this cause a further distancing from others. I understood the pain in the physical body that Mother Teresa spoke about when she walked through the streets of Calcutta without finding any food or shelter. What I should be and what I wasn't being was a haunting refrain. What I was seeing for the first time were those who were as hungry as I was on the streets. I never noticed those who were homeless in the same way before for now I was one of them. The cultural differentials are a complex separator. When one is hungry, "otherness" disappears, and only one experience remains intact and that is the universal knowledge that everyone needs to eat to live. I thought how interesting it would be if we, as a global community, could enter a solidarity of fasting, such as Ramadan which is honored in the religion of Islam. Here Muslims everywhere take into account their neighbors, friends, and acquaintances and become mindful of this serious human condition that hunger creates as a participatory synchronicity of reality.

Hungry, exhausted, and depressed, as I walked further in the night talking out loud to myself, and demeaning myself for obsessive self-cherishing, I noticed a sign on the side of a building asking for help as a night clerk in what looked like a rooming house in San Francisco. I heard an inner voice say, "What is nourishment anyway?" I was stunned by this inner question, as it seemed a bigger issue than just simply thinking of food to eat to fill my stomach. Attempting to find an answer to this question, I stood there frozen, staring into the building trying to see something through the "Night Clerk needed" job sign for something profound, anything that would make sense. For a sudden moment, I was standing in an open and willing state knowing how susceptible the body is to all changes and conditions and yet something in me was set free from this feeling of hunger and loneliness. I later understood and will paraphrase a particular Iya in Holy Qur'an that I remember: *"God is free from all wants, it is you (the personal ego identity) who is needy."* Most of our real work is beyond the realm of the ego as that was the moment I set my sentinel at the door of perception to become cognizant of my thoughts through observation.

Still looking at the sign and building, somewhat immobile in my body, I recalled a kind of familiarity about this place but no information about the hotel, which looked unexceptional from all outer appearances, but I eventually put one foot in front of the other and went into the front office. I talked to the young man who ran the place. He was friendly and open and not very interested about learning where I came from or about my situation. I found he simply was sensing my character as we entered a verbal exchange about my ability to work night shifts versus days. When I said I had no trouble with working nights, he hired me and requested I work for no salary, but I would be given room and board in exchange for work. I accepted the arrangement.

Working as the night shift concierge for several weeks, I noticed the residents were mostly men who occupied the rooms. I would see police officers in the lobby during the evening hours that I had my shift. I came to understand that I had been hired on in a halfway house for ex-convicts. In this halfway house, it was a preparation for me to learn about the men who had little time to figure out how to make their way back into society, back into their families and their communities, and a preparation for them to figure things out.

My developing awareness about cultural isolation, loneliness, and incarceration took a massive leap forward as I developed friendships with these men. I later took a job, thanks to Bo Lozoff, as the Director of the Prison Library Project for five years, serving the men and their families who were "*doing time on the inside*." I supplied spiritual literature for their libraries, read to them, and counseled them. Their stories were filled with regret and anger and reflected their stubbornness to change as they shared their problems that brought them into self-imposed starvation of one kind or another.

My experience as a night shift concierge gave me the practicum to act under oppressive circumstances and offered meaning as to why empathy is so important. In later years, after meeting Mother Teresa at the Mission of Charities in San Francisco, I traveled to Calcutta leading a group of Sufi women offering our service to Mother Teresa's establishment in the Kalighat, the center for the dying. There I gained transcendental insight into the experience of cultural isolation, hunger, and death. The condition of homelessness is the same in Calcutta as it is in San Francisco. Sadly, it seems our eyes in the Western hemisphere are closed to this level of suffering, and if they are open, we seem to refuse to act with compassion. I understood how men on parole offered an accurate representation of a marginalized group. Black, Hispanic, and White young men who were aimlessly seeking for some fragment of greater creative freedom in the physical world as they lacked the tools for bringing their creative impulses from the abstract to the manifest. During a temporary period of my youth, I, too, was disassociated from members of my family and community. I could not return to the comfort of my past existence either, though I re-engaged with my family later on as these aspects of separation became clear to me. I came to realize that I had found utter synchronicity about homelessness as I was a prisoner in the cell of my illusionary separation, starving for spiritual nourishment, and now I was united with a group of men who came from a similar jail. As Bo Lozoff has profoundly said, *"We are all doing time."*[xii]

If Mother Teresa found sympathetic resonance with homeless people, whom she was compelled to serve because she too remembered in her body awareness what homelessness felt like, how much greater her story prepares us for finding consilience in all degrees of starvation and homelessness in our lives. I found a mutual sanctuary as well with those men who had a similar experience of deprivation and famine but not necessarily the kind that Mother Teresa exposed to the world in her work in Calcutta. Those whom Mother Teresa served shared the same sense of abandonment by the social system in which they were born into as she did, only her protection was the Catholic Church; but her options indicated she would not return to those protections. In her simple act of social justice, which was in reality hard manual labor, and following her sensing of what it was to be homeless and hungry, which were the same painful physical sensations that told her not to return to the convent, she changed the world's view of the poor by remaining in the same condition. This was a brave action by an independent missionary.

Having had the opportunity of working with Mother Teresa both in the San Francisco Mission of Charities and in Calcutta, I came to understand something about her prophetic nature that was always in a state of respect and remembrance of Jesus and his work with the poor. I viewed her work and testimony to her love of Jesus not as the historic Jesus the man, her work with the poor around the world took the form of Jesus as a Christéd Mother, caretaker, and servant by doing what was needed for those who require care and a loving hand. She developed the natural talent and practical mastery of embodying the Divine Holy Mother's energy and spirit in her actions although her personality remained clearly hard-driving and persistent. She was a master of listening and would not easily be dissuaded to turn away from her sensing nature, which appeared to always care for the Divine in others. She often quoted this phrase from the Bible, "*I was naked and you gave me clothing, I was sick, and you cared for me, I was in prison, and you visited me.*" [xiii] I perceived she followed this saying as a guiding rule in all her actions.

I remember a distinctive day when the new Mission of Charity opened in San Francisco. Right before we were scheduled to open the doors to the lines of waiting, hungry and homeless men and women standing out in the cold street during the winter months when the wind was severe and icy, an odd person appeared on the scene. A representative from the Building Code came to inspect the water heater to make sure everything was up to code regulations for the opening. After a lengthy inspection with three of us standing there, he announced that the heating system was antiquated and not usable and needed to be replaced. After a long silence, Mother Teresa asked how much another heater would be and what was the timing necessary for the installation of the new one? The Code fellow went into an in-depth explanation of the bureaucratic nightmare of permissions offering a three-month marker (perhaps) for delivery and installation of a new system after the State coding laws were approved, and another month to replace the heater. He quoted the cost of about $500,000 or more, if I remember correctly his estimate for replacement of the system and labor. Mother Teresa just listened and remained silent, no reactions were apparent on her face, but this time her glance became internal and she was still for what felt like elongated minutes stretching into hours. Then she swiftly turned to the sister standing next to me and said in declarative authority, *"Take it out!"* and walked out of the room. The Code fellow was aghast. *"What did she say?"* he asked. Shrugging her shoulders almost apologetically, Sister said, *"Take it out!"* This we did! A demolition crew was called in almost immediately, and the old heating system was stripped from the building. The next day we were open to offer a bed and hot meals to those who were waiting on the streets for the exact opening time promised. We only had cold water to use for washing but our soups were hot and the meals were plentiful because of previous donations. There was no code to worry about and people were kept warm with multiple blankets.

I thought a great deal about that situation and I tried to see what Mother Teresa was looking at in her silence. Was she looking for strategies that the City Code fellow would accept? Was she wondering where the money was going to come from to pay for a heating system? Quite frankly, I don't think these thoughts ever entered her consciousness. I believe she was acting from an immediate realization of how the Divine Presence serves those who are starving, homeless, and cold in the immediate moment. In the simplest and most direct manner, she was back into the inner state of her moments of hunger and homelessness, and completely united with all those people waiting on line. Her mastery was her intentionality to carry out a task in such an effective, persuasive way that gave reverence to who she was holding in her heart. She was transmitting what she would have wanted and needed when she was homeless and hungry. Mother Teresa exemplifies in her actions how the great Holy Mother-Gaia works in the world when Her Being moves into our interiority. One can say, it is like a solution to a hermeneutic characteristic, something distant required closer proximity, a certain strangeness overcome, a bridge was built between the once and the now. [xiv] The Holy Mother of the World-Gaia creates relationships to guide the way whether the relationship is from past to present, or present to future. This experience reveals a glorious consilience of awareness. What comes into your heart when you read about this? Have you ever had an experience of being homeless, hungry, and alone?

Noor-un-nisa Inayat Khan (1914-1943) -The Willing Self-Sacrifice

Noor-un-nisa Inayat Khan was born in Moscow, Russia, on January 1, 1914 to the saintly Indian Sufi mystic Hazrat Inayat Khan and Ora Ray Baker, an American from Albuquerque, New Mexico. Baker was the grandniece of Mary Baker Eddy, who began the Church of Christian Science. Her father, Hazrat Inayat Khan, was raised in India in a family of musicians and Sufi Mystics. Refined musical artists, painters, and poets who were trained in the great esoteric traditions of the Eastern world surrounded him.

His esoteric work brought synthesis to four major Sufi Tariqats (lineages): the Suhrwardi, Naqshabandi, Qadiri, and Chisti Orders. Although learned in the traditional Sufi Principles of these four schools of esoteric thought, his Message of Love, Harmony, and Beauty brought a new impulse to the West as he offered teachings on Spiritual Liberty breaking away from any conservative, doctrinal systems that would try to claim the new mystical Message held sacredly by the Sufi Movement International, an organization he created during his life. Inayat Khan honored the prophets that brought spiritual teachings into the world and established a unified principle for which all beings would respect and learn from the sacred traditions. He called this activity the Unity of Religious Ideals. Through generous and mindful consideration for the many belief systems, he wanted to move into the future free of codified religious behavior that proliferated insularity. As he prepared his Victorian students to receive the Sufi Message of Spiritual Liberty and the Unity of Spiritual Ideals that was expounded years before its time, his personal life also changed. He married Ora Ray Baker and fathered four beautiful children who all received an element of his mystically awakened being. Noor-un-nisa was his first daughter.

Noor-un-nisa was regarded as a sensitive and shy individual with dreamy aspirations. She studied child psychology at the Sorbonne and music at the Paris Conservatory, specializing in harp and piano with the famous teacher, Nadia Boulanger.

When her father died in 1927, she took care of her brothers and sister and took over the mothering of her mother, who retreated to bed in despair at the death of her husband. It was a very unstable emotional time for Noor-un-nisa and the whole family. Yet during that period she wrote a well-published book for children, the *Jataka Tales,* stories of the Buddha's many incarnations as animals. The book reveals valuable insight into her delicate heart and soul as she articulates mystical understanding absorbed through her father's profound esoteric transmission to her and also a prediction concerning her own sacrifice.

When World War II broke out and France became overrun with Nazi troops in 1940, the family fled to London. Noor-un-nisa was a pacifist by inherited teachings of her father and was deeply conflicted about how to help in this untenable situation. Her brother, Vilayat, recorded a benefit and not to collude with injustice through passivity. Vilayat stated,

On the eve of the war, Noor and I conferred deeply and at length on the pros and cons of our participation in the war. The problem was the same question asked today by conscientious objectors. We had been formed at the school of our Father, an Eastern sage and teacher. Behind him lay the entire tradition of Eastern spirituality. The then budding Gandhi inspired a non-violent campaign and had proven its effectiveness as a means of confronting violence but was barely explored in the West. And was this not the message of Christ? Was there not a contradiction in killing in order to stop manslaughter? But suppose a Nazi should hold hostages at gunpoint and starve them to death; it would be complicity to their murder if, having the means to kill the Nazi and unable to otherwise prevent him from carrying out his deed, we abstain from doing it in the name of non-violence. As we had that conversation, could we have ever imagined that one day Noor would find herself in the plight of the people she wanted to save? [xv]

After being assigned to a bomber training school in June 1941, she applied for a commission in an attempt to relieve herself of the boring work there. Later she was recruited to join F (France) Section of the Special Operations Executive, and in early February 1943 she was posted to the Air Ministry, section Directorate of Air Intelligence, seconded to First Aid Nursing Yeomanry (FANY), and sent to Wanborough Manor, near Guildford in Surrey. From there she was sent to various other SOE schools for training, including STS 5 Winterfold, STS 36 Boarmans, and STS 52 Thame Park. During her training she adopted the name Nora Baker. Her training was incomplete, and her superiors held mixed opinions on her suitability for secret warfare. Nevertheless, her fluency in French and her competency in wireless operation—coupled with a shortage of experienced agents—made her a desirable candidate for service in Nazi-occupied France.

In June of 1943 she was given a cryptonym "Madeleine" W/T operator "Nurse" and, under the cover identity of Jeanne-Marie Regnier, Assistant Section Officer/Ensign Inayat Khan was flown to landing ground B/20A "Indigestion" in Northern France on a night landing double Lysander operation, code-named Teacher/Nurse/Chaplain/Monk. Henri Dericourt met her.

She traveled to Paris, and together with two other women (Diane Rowden, code name Paulette/Chaplain, and Cecily Lefort, code name Alice/Teacher), Noor joined the Physician network led by Francis Suttill, code name Prosper.

Over the next month and a half, the Sicherheitsdienst (SD) arrested all other Physician network radio operators. In spite of the danger, Noor rejected an offer to return to Britain, and she continued transmitting as the last essential link between London and Paris.

Moving from place to place, she managed to escape capture while maintaining wireless communication with London. "She refused however to abandon what had become the principal and most dangerous post in France . . . and did . . . excellent work" (Central Chancery of the Orders of Knighthood, 1949).

On or about October 13, 1943, Noor-un-nisa Inayat Khan was arrested and interrogated at the SD Headquarters at 84 Avenue Foch in Paris. She appeared so gentle and unworldly that the SOE trainers became fiercely afraid of her and treated her as an extremely dangerous prisoner. She would say, *"You cannot take from me that which you know not."* [xvi] Her interrogation lasted a full month. She attempted an escape twice but was captured immediately in the same vicinity. She was taken to Germany on

November 27, 1943 for safe custody and imprisoned in Pforsheim in solitary confinement with no contact with the outside world.

She was chained to the cement floor and tortured continually by being brutally beaten with a stick and whipped by a sadistic SS guard Wilhelm Ruppert before being shot in the back of the head. Her last words were *"Vive La Liberté."* [xvii]

Noor-un-nisa Inayat Khan was posthumously awarded a British Mention in Dispatches and a French Croix de Guerre with Gold Star. She was the third WWII FANY member to be awarded the George Cross, Britain's highest award for gallantry not on the battlefield. [xviii]

Correlation

No single experience could identify the difficulties that many individuals endured during WWII except those who were there in the trenches themselves, yet there is a somatic sensing in the heart that knows about war. The war that Noor-un-nisa experienced was founded on domination, hatred, and bigotry, and yet there are correlations of experience and many kinds of wars as Philo of Alexandra (20 B.C.-40 A.D) said, *"Everyone we meet is fighting a great battle."* Wars are fought on many levels, and in my generation, which is the 21st century, one of our great leaders in the USA, Martin Luther King Jr., reminded us how *"the arc of the moral universe is long, but it bends toward justice."* Indeed Noor-un-nisa's act of self-sacrifice revealed a profound inner arc of an ancient spirit. MLK's comment brings insight to

Noor-un-nisa's narrative, as her intentional experience was *"noetic"* as it is in itself offering an intuitive meaning and becomes more meaningful as it continues to reveal a deeper sacred significance *"noesis."* [xix] Her deeper meaning was precognitive and revealed in one of Noor-un-nisa's children's stories from her book that I paraphrase, in the *Jataka Tales* about the Great Elephant.

The Great Elephant who is happy and out dancing among the banana trees watching blissfully the day and night in the desert arose in my experience as an ideal that knew his time for inner change was coming. One day the Great Elephant hears strange voices and realizes how unhappy the cries of humans are. *"Why are they crying and why are they so unhappy?"* He begins walking toward the crying sounds and finally came across a large crowd of people walking in the desert, looking like they were going to die. With empathy and emotion he asks the travelers why they came to this desert and how he might help them. Deeply moved by his kindness, the people knelt before him telling him their story of being chased away from their homes by a despotic King. They tell him they have been walking for days and nights without food or water and during their long journey many have died, especially the children.

The Great Elephant realized as he looked around seeing only human beings starving that they could not go much longer, as the next village was too far. He told them of a stream and about the body of a great elephant that they could eat just a few miles away down the road. After saying this he ran away and disappeared. The people were perplexed at this news but followed his instructions. When they arrived at the stream, they saw the great elephant at the bottom of the high hill dead near the stream of water the Great Elephant had spoken about. But as they went up closer to the elephant, they noticed in horror that it was the very dear Great Elephant they had met on the road who sacrificed his life. Many of the people said they would not eat it but the wise elders said, *"If we do not eat this elephant, his sacrifice will have been useless, and we shall die before reaching the city. We will not be helped and the wishes of the Great Elephant will not have been fulfilled."* All ate the meat with tears in their eyes and it made them strong so that they could reach the next village. [xx]

This *Jataka Tale* opens a deep question about how one might value dying for a purpose. Most mothers would lay down their lives for the life of their child. But to lay down one's life for the women, men, and children of a village that one does not know, as Noor-un-nisa did, knowing that the Nazis would catch her, was indeed the ultimate gift of self-sacrifice and an action that was precognitive and reiterated in the Great Elephant story.

We will never know the exact circumstances of her experiences, but hearing her story from her brother's information and the *Jataka Tale* about the Great Elephant provided a framework for a difficult decision that paired with mine when under a life-threatening situation. The following moment rose up in consilience as I felt the scene enter once again, like a moving picture, into reality as I reflected on Noor-un-nisa's experiences.

Consilience

I was working for an NGO and riding in a truck in the Somali terrain with a team of medical workers, bringing food and medicine into refugee camps. Young terrorists about the age of 14 abruptly held up the supply trucks, containing medicine and food for 25,000 refugees. They aggressively pointed guns at the entire group, and ordered all the U.S. workers to disembark. We did not know what would unfold, but it did not look like it was going to be a good day. I experienced our collective destiny going blank for one quintessential moment, which felt like an eternity. Sitting on the side of the road in the burning sun, we watched these young Somali brigands dismantle our trucks of the food and medicines meant for their own people. They threw valuable equipment to the ground and scattered the contents in a chaotic manner. As I thought of the 25,000 refugees who needed these supplies, my thoughts tried to make sense of an unethical paradox. I was witnessing the same members of that starving community we were attempting to assist, and here they were robbing from themselves.

"Is this the time to face my own death the way Noor-un-nisa had to face hers?" I asked myself. *"If I act in some way antagonistic to these young men, will I get myself and others killed? Would my death somehow bring greater urgency to the plight of a starving nation of people?"* These thoughts rambled through my head as I felt I had to quickly come to terms with dying today in Africa, now or very soon. I understood there was not much time. What difference does it make if I do something or nothing? What can one obscure person from the West do to change the difficult fate of millions in the African nation wrecked hopelessly by colonialism, drought, and corruption? I was so perplexed, and my adrenaline was pumping. Just thinking I could perhaps do "something good" in the immediate thought that would make my death more purposeful brought a lessening of fear about being killed, a feeling that everything, even if I died, would be OK. What could be my positive last thoughts? This existential feeling seemed to bring a hidden relief to my physical body and a sense of spaciousness arose. I also felt fulfillment in doing work such as bringing in food and medicines from the West that I truly believed was a helpful contribution to the immediate famine crisis, although I knew intuitively it was not a long-term answer to the suffering. Somehow...out of spaciousness, a sacred fearlessness arose to just let everything unfold as it will.

As I sat on the road, all the trees had been stripped away and the desert road was open and wide. I could easily see a leader of the young brigands identifying himself by the way he was shouting orders to the others who were younger. Very slowly, I positioned myself near him with careful attention to making my last words on earth the best words I could muster under the circumstances, I blurted out, *"What do you think about Bob Marley's music?"* He looked as stunned as I was by the question, and he began to smile. *"I like Bob Marley,"* he replied in broken English, and his rifle pointed slowly to the ground. We began to talk about music and sang together, *"One World, One Heart, Let's get together and we'll be alright."* After singing and laughing as we repeated the magical reggae refrain, the musical conversation merged into negotiation, and I convinced him to take only half of the food and medical load. This was a fitting negotiation, as the young brigands did not have the trucks they needed anyway, and killing all of us would have created an international incident of such political proportion they would not have had time to profit from the robbery; and it must be noted they too were under adult manipulation and they could have been killed by those who controlled them if they did not bring back the loot.

Could the brilliance of that moment so precisely recorded in my memory, and the outcome with a 14-year-old boy, who had a gun but no future, no food, and no home, work out to benefit all of us, the group of medical workers and the refugees? I can only guess that his survival exposed no future at all except a life of despotic actions controlled by adults that were causing him to act in such a manner. If, during that incident, my own feelings sensed my days on earth were to end, could the same momentary synchronicity of a self-sacrifice for a cause greater than one's own life have been the reason that gave me the inspiration to call out Bob Marley's song? When I contemplate

Noor-un-nisa's choice to remain at her post as radio operator, she saved the lives of many women, men, and children. By giving her life away willingly as a generous sacrifice to an oppressive force that could never understand the nature of secret spirituality that drove her soul, Noor-un-nisa upheld the actions of the Holy Mother-Gaia's willing sacrifice for her children, as Her main purpose is to protect Her creation.

Like the Great Elephant, she fed herself to others so that the greater group may thrive. Her own death for a cause she believed was worth the ultimate sacrifice. Was not one life a worthy exchange if it saved many?

For years I have been aware about Noor-un-nisa's life because of my Sufi associations. I knew both her brothers and spoke to them about her decision to remain in full integrity when human hatred turned against her. Paired to a time when my life was in the tenuous hands of young, ignorant boys produced a viable option for success. The past and the present "paired" in an inextricable variation on a theme, and that was the threat of life under a gun. The circumstances were different, but my innate responses in the desert of Africa held true to my intuitive feelings of accomplishing a mission as Noor-un-nisa's did as a radio operator. Perhaps music linked Noor-un-nisa and me. Most certainly the love for her father, Hazrat Inayat Khan, and the great mystical teachings he brought to the world, connected our hearts together beyond time and space. Noor-un-nisa's self-sacrifice somehow made it easier for me to hold the conscious mind in a tenuous state of ease rather than in fear when being threatened. Just knowing Noor-un-nisa's story opened a greater vista from which to make choices. The team and I did successfully transport the rest of the medicines and food into the medical camp and returned home back to the USA safely.

Other aspects of synchronicity mystically paired with Noor-un-nisa's life choices, particularly the idea of joining military service. I recalled several dreams I had that united me to an awareness of a soldier's ultimate duty, and another dream which was precognitive that manifested in reality years later all having to do with military uniforms.

The first dream I recorded, when I was very young, around the age of 9 years old, involved a scene where I am standing on a pier by the ocean on a foggy, cold night in Europe. I was wearing a brown military uniform speaking French intently to a senior officer about an activity I was about to perform in a secret mission. The nature of the information was not clear in the dream; it was rather the hyper-intensity of the moment, the visceral sensing of danger that overshadowed the meeting. There was an ominous feeling that surrounded this meeting. The profound seriousness of our conversation lingered. My dream repeated many times over the years from my youth to my adulthood. It was paired to the moment when I found myself in Africa with the medical team. We were not wearing a prescribed uniform but we were in khakis that looked similar and our mission united us.

The second dream occurred in France. I was a grade school teacher during WWII who was trying to transfer the children in my second-story classroom downstairs to the street into a bomb shelter. The air-raid sirens were going off and I knew the danger in each moment. I had to find all the children and get them to the shelter. I could hear the bombs dropping close by. As I was leading the children across the street, to the shelter, a young boy cried out from the second-story window who appeared very frightened. I knew I had to go back for him. Just as I turned to run across the street to the school entry, I saw a young man walking toward me in an American pilot's uniform. He understood the urgency and assessed the situation immediately. I turned to him and we looked at each other for an intense moment and in his eyes I saw an eternal connection that I did not understand at the time but this brought me a deep sense of calm. He knew intuitively what we needed to do. We ran into the building together and as we reached the boy, the bomb dropped on the school and we were all killed. In the consilience of this scene, I met the pilot again in my present life and he became my husband, Robin Julien Laflamme, to whom this book is dedicated. The interesting connection to the dream was Robin knew all about the WWII airplanes and remembers flying them in past memories and, if given the opportunity, he could fly one in the present day without having had any instructions.

It is well known and understood that dreams portend the innate awareness that comes when one acts altruistically and wears a uniform of responsibility representing their Nation or group. It is an honorary mantle when such a priestly robe is worn, or a shawl of light placed on one's shoulders is given, revealing a duty that is bestowed upon an individual. When these outer garments are worn, the individual must live by the Sacred Spirit that directs them now and forever. The inherent code in the mantle of responsibility entails an ethical agreement with an individual in which a promise to defend and serve all life for the hope of a greater good, whether externalized or internalized, is taken. To be a member of a military group that offers the idea of a social change from fascist domination to freedom, or a spiritual robe that a sacred ideal of unity is possible in the human condition against the destruction of life and freedom, is a germinating seed that illuminates the inner essence of how the Divine Mother serves her creation within any social grouping. This impulse is identified in a code as "Protection of the Nation's Soul" meaning the "people." This is found in the refined level of

44

responsibility that all soldiers and spiritual practitioners make in their hearts. These are the reflections that came to me when I entered the life story of Noor-un-nisa. What arises in your consciousness?

Reverend Amanuensis Frida Waterhouse (1907-1987) - The Gadfly

Frida Waterhouse was born of Jewish parents on October 12, 1907 at Gloversville, New York, and she died on November 18, 1987. The year 1907 was the prelude to an economic depression in the United States, and there was barely any food in the house for the family of four. Both parents became very ill and the children were sent away into the care of two adults who traumatized them with beatings, rape, and violent actions such as locking them in closets. When the family came back together a few years later, they moved to Los Angeles.

Though the mother and father remained in fragile health, they both joined the Young People's Socialist League and brought the young girls with them to the meetings. Frida remained active in this organization until the age of 19. The discussions that took place at the meetings imbued her with a desire to serve her fellow human beings. She was insistent to question authority and political leaders, and this activated a rebellious sense of identity. She had a difficult time conforming to the status quo found in feminine socialization of her time. The limitation and subjugation of a woman's role, which was relegated to serving a male and producing children, completely diminished her sense of identity, realizing at the same time it might serve other women's needs if they chose it freely. She endured constant limitations when applying for jobs. A repetitive pattern she witnessed was how men always held important positions of authority. Frida became fiercely angry when a male person talked down to her as though she was ignorant and uneducated when her intellect was far superior to those with whom she was applying for work.

She took odd jobs to survive and decided to have a common law relationship instead of marrying. Later she did marry, but the relationship was not successful although it lasted 13 years. She attempted to follow the expected patterns for women and stay in the status quo, but she could not stand it. After separation and divorce she considered this action the single most important factor that moved her toward her spiritual goals. She ended her relationship so skillfully and with great compassion. She invited her husband to a dinner that she paid for, bought him a present, and thanked him for being a wonderful man in her life. Telling him all she remembered about his sterling qualities, she asked him to release her as his wife and let her go. He did so with graciousness and love.

While living in Los Angeles, she enjoyed sharing stimulating discussions with her mother and father. The family loved to discuss politics, music, and literature, but her inner self-discovery became an important motivation for her to separate from family and move to San Francisco to begin a new life.

Her anguish over the breakup of her marriage and the onset of a genetic inheritance of cataracts in both eyes caused her to become blind. She did not submit to surgery at that time because of the unknown factors surrounding the surgical procedure, but most importantly she was guided by her intuition to remain blind so that she could develop inner sensitivities. She attained what she called *"important levels of spiritual insight"* born from her decision to remain blind for the duration of 4 to 5 years, a period she indicated developed her inner awareness. This period became clearer as her insight became keenly focused and she began to listen with great intensity. [xxi]

The nature of her work was to provide a practical springboard to help others adjust to active and reactive spiritual changes. She offered counseling to people between the years 1972 and 1986. The spiritual force fields surrounding an individual's Dharma (Spiritual-Soul) path were her focus when working in one-to-one settings. She called her vibrant inner work a meeting of the Three Selves of our Being. The Three Selves included the Basic Selves, the Conscious self, and the High Self or Divine image of God that one was reflecting in their inner consciousness. (The following sections are abstracted from her book, *Why Me.*) [xxii]

Frida revealed the Three Selves by first tracking how the High Self researches one's Akashic record (or the inner history of karmic patterns) to see what you as a soul force have accomplished or what its failures have been in the past. Together with one's individual soul blueprint, and the free will of the person, it can guide the person unerringly towards the spiritual goals for this lifetime. The High Self is not you! Frida understood the High Self as an entity at a higher spiral of spiritual evolution that has volunteered to come in and act as one's guide and teacher. It may have come from another planet or graduated from the earth plane as a basic self. It has its own wisdom and is the gateway to the Divine understanding. [xxiii]

The High Self can also reach through to the planetary Akasha, or what Carl Jung call the *"collective unconscious,"* to obtain data on all creative thought, poetry, music, mathematics, and inventions and bring it back to you for practical use. Frida found during her sessions with others that the High Self may be seated in one's crown chakra, or it can be attached or connected to some other part of one's etheric double (etheric body). Since it operates under the law of a human being's free will, it will not force its guidance upon the person. However, if one invites it to do so, and graciously considers what is offered, it will keep one's feet unerringly on one's spiritual plan. The High Self will closely follow the individual blueprint for this lifetime and help an individual toward fulfilling the ultimate plan for the soul. [xxiv]

Frida repeatedly indicated that the ideas presented in a session are not ultimatums or doctrines written in stone. The information offered can be accepted or rejected by the person according to their evolution to understand esoteric principles operating in their lives. The esoteric principles that an individual needed to understand where those Martin Buber articulated in his book, *For the Sake of Heaven*, in which free choice was accepted as one's remaining defiant choice or one's willingness to change. Whatever path the soul sets forth toward their ultimate destiny, the personality-consciousness will reap the consequences of its actions.

As Frida offered her dedicated work over the many years, seeing hundreds of people including State dignitaries, she understood how a person's High Self is the part of the "Super-conscious structure" and is the Divine Mind. It is the gateway to Samadhi (state of bliss) and opens guidance to a persona consciousness from teachers on the inner planes. It is the doorway through which one can reach the Creator. It is one's ultimate spiritual teacher. The earth plane teachers are simply guiding individuals to get one to their High Self teacher. Frida always laughed when she said, "*Symbolically speaking the High Self can save you many a bloody nose, skinned knees or even major fractures."*

The High Self also acts as a transformer, stepping down the energies of spiritual force fields that seek to guide or teach one how to balance and integrate arising information that might not be understood at the moment it appears. If these energies were allowed to come straight through, they might shatter one's mind and body.

In other words, Frida said, *"the High Self selected YOU, the type of body, sex, time and place of birth, one's parents who are chosen for their strengths and weaknesses and sisters and brothers. The High Self chooses everything that has to do with promoting one's ultimate soul's plan."* [xxv] Frida always reminded those she worked with her that most individuals have volunteered to come into the earth cycle by one's free will and therefore one must take full responsibility for the whole plan. That means no blame for yourself, your parents, or toward your whole familial situation. While Frida found it was true that one was not consulted about the details of their blueprint, one made the tacit agreement to help it come into fruition. [xxvi]

Working with the High Self is the Personality Consciousness that has the privilege of acting out the daily dramas and challenges on the stage of life. Frida termed this *"the reasoning mind,"* which can proceed from a premise to a conclusion. The reality behind the on-stage action is that the purpose of the action is solely for lesson learning--nothing else. When the action is *"freaking a person out,"* one can rebalance and come back much sooner if one faces the lesson that is necessary for the moment. If a person runs away, refusing to learn the lessons, you just end up coming back to do it another time. Frida always asked everyone that worked with her, *"Why not do the work now rather than wait and procrastinate?"* One is on earth to fulfill the Divine blueprint that was given to the individual. Whether one takes the lesson or refuses to learn it as this is always a free choice, but Frida asked that we be courageous and face our ultimate demons and dragons. She felt that being courageous always helped individuals move toward a happier life. A happier life was found when one lived in a greater expansive state and used the attributes of generosity, respect, love, and empathetic responsiveness without fear.

Lastly, Frida indicated that the High Self selects a basic self from a repository within the inner planes. She found this to be an entity that is not the individual, per se. The basic self enters shortly after conception while in the mother's womb. It is an entity of a lower spiral of spiritual evolution and is located in the physical area of one's solar plexus. Frida called this the *"subjective mind."* In her work with others, she found there could be more than one basic self, such as a feminine and masculine entity. These female and male entities come in to redeem their own karmic patterns and raise themselves in their own evolution by helping the personality-consciousness achieve its plan. In other words, as the personality consciousness helps the soul move up on its own spiral of evolution so does the subconscious mind, providing they both cooperate with one another.

She found in application, through the Three Self method, that consciousness has never been a basic self. However, she found it was possible for the basic self to make a quantum leap by becoming a High Self, and this occurred by neutralizing its own negativities and cooperating with the conscious self in fulfilling the soul's blueprint. This synchronicity happened when all parts of the Self moved into harmony.

The High Self, the conscious self, and the basic selves are separate entities that have the right of free will, likes and dislikes, and the ability to accept or reject the flow of karmic patterns. The karmic patterns flow through the High Self, bypassing the conscious self, and go directly to the basic selves or subconscious mind. They are activated there, complete with memory patterns of prior times, and are referred up to the conscious level to be worked out.

As evidenced in her work with hundreds of individuals, Frida found that at certain times, the basic selves would block an individual's progress. The basic selves might not believe in God and they have the right not to. It might not accept the karmic pattern or even think there is such a thing as karmic law. Therefore, if there are guilt patterns within the karmic patterns that should be flowing to the conscious self to be transmuted in this time and place, it will block them off. The basic selves are there to serve as the lower mind, the least developed of the three minds, to permit a pattern to flow. In the lower mind, great transformation can take place. It is where the ego-nature can be completely restructured to serve the higher purpose of the individual. This transformation can take place without bias or dualism pitting one aspect against another. The transformation provides a cooperative harmonic experience for the individual that is not based on preferences but rather develops neutrality. Neutrality is the state one can enter when belligerent thoughts no longer capsize the consciousness.

Her work brought her closer to the gender argument that many people in the gay/lesbian community were experiencing through a degraded social form known as gay-bashing and hatred of gender identification. Some aspects of Religious doctrine were declaring that homosexuality was a sickness and a perversion. Frida's response to this type of profiling was revolutionary and gave impulse for wider understanding in the 1960s and 1970s. Frida believed that subconscious mind can be either masculine or feminine within either a male or a female physical body and they have distinct characteristics such as strength, will, and determination for a male and love, warmth, emotion, and sensitivity for a female entity. This was one of the reasons why she never judged what theological practitioners were calling "*sexual deviation*," as she did not find these exhibitions of entity qualities a deviation at all but rather the reflection of the exact purpose that the Divine plan was enabling the karmic patterns in an individual to be carried out. She was one of the first advocates in the Bay Area who openly protested against marginalized bigotry of the LGBT community. In active response, she formed regular group meetings for gay men's empowerment and women's empowerment through the exploration of their entity forces.

These classes went on for years to help the gay members ride out the tsunami of negative energy they were dealing with from society. She remained committed all her life to the open discussion of these matters and spoke at many religious communities so that education about the Three Selves might take place and help change the unconscious programming that fundamentally supported hatred and marginalization. Frida's work was confirmed years later after her death when the research of Dr. Dean Hamer, who is an AIDS researcher at the U.S. National Cancer Institute near Washington, D.C., research an amazing series of studies indicating the genetic proclivity of the X chromosome. Dr. Hamer studied the family histories of 114 homosexuals and found that 13.5% of the gay men's brothers were also homosexual, compared with 2% in the general population. They also found maternal uncles and maternal male cousins were more likely to be homosexual. In some families, gay relatives could be traced back three generations. Because homosexual uncles and male cousins of the gay persons were raised in different households, the scientists hypothesized a genetic factor on the X chromosome, known as Xq28. In brief, the scientific research implies that being gay or

53

straight relies to some extent on a genetic predisposition. Researchers can only speculate on what the gene does or does not do, and scientists have indications of how environmental factors and life experience, traumatic or other, may have affected the disposition of those who are homosexual. [xxvii]

Frida's work clearly establishes an integration of spirituality, psychology, and the body. She honored the ancient Hawaiian Kahuna teachings, and was the leading forerunner of the Three Selves method before the published texts of Max Freedom Long years later. She incorporated the Christian teachings advocated by the Universal Church of the Master, which became the umbrella organization to allow her to function as Reverend and a ministerial counselor.

The Universal Church of the Master was an organization founded in Santa Clara, California in 1908 that supported the study and diffusion of spiritual truths found in history, mundane and arcane sciences, spiritual and natural philosophy, occultism, astrology, psychometrics, parapsychology, and theology. The community respected pluralistic study but focused on the study of Christian principles as found in the Aquarian Gospel of Jesus Christ. The teaching in the Aquarian Gospel reflects the essential appeal to return to the teachings of Jesus that could only be understood when the Aquarian rising time of people's consciousness desired transformation and when they were ready to place into action esoteric spiritual principles rather than dogma. In the Aquarian Gospel, Jesus said to his disciples, *"I have many things to say unto you, but you cannot bear them now. Howbeit when she, the Spirit of Truth, is come she will guide you into all truth."* [xxviii] Frida felt guided by this comment of the Master Jesus as she knew from her lived experience and from working with so many individuals, people could only awaken when they are ready and willing to work in harmony with the destiny

54

pattern that had been given to them individually and to the society at large. She felt that everyone on the planet came into the earth plane together for a greater purpose as we were a part of a larger plan of developing consciousness than that of national boundaries, which political representatives from all nations tried to divide.

Correlation

I worked with Frida for over 15 years and I understood Frida's philosophical system somatically when I was fortunate enough to conduct a pilgrimage to Egypt with a group of Sufi practitioners. As we walked in the Valley of the Queens, the mass of people walking on the prescribed tracks to and from the monument to Queen Hatshepsut, offered an indelible experience as I caught the glance of the people passing me. It was familiar. I felt as though we, the mass of moving beings, were all returning to the place we all came from originally. It was a momentary awareness, yet somatically full of reverence. In the past, crowds of people agitated me but this crowd of people brought great awareness and comfort to my soul remembrance. I felt embraced by a community I welcomed again into my immediate presence.

Frida prepared students to respect experiential teachings however they arose, such as the one expressed above, and for all teachers both inner and outer, the Holy Prophets, Angels, and Saints that guided them, and the inner working of the Three Selves within one's consciousness. She felt that connectedness through respect and listening forged an intuitive development that prepared an individual to meet the exigencies arising in one's life. She never promised success or advanced the idea to grasp for an outcome or any initiation into a major spiritual role. She simply offered a tool kit that brought communication within oneself and a heightening of intuitive skills in the hopes of setting one's foot unerringly onto the path of spirit.

A seemingly mundane incident that Frida conveyed one day during our 15-year relationship gives evidence to the power of her insight and intuition.

Frida suffered from scoliosis, a bone degeneration that curved the spinal column and caused her to remain bent and with a slight hump on the left rear portion of her back. After eye surgery that enabled her to see, she had to wear very thick glasses, which caused her beautiful clear blue eyes to appear quite large when gazing frontally at her face. She was very small (4'8") and thin, and had white hair, which she pulled back in a ponytail with a small fringe of bangs. She always walked slowly supported by a black lacquered cane with a green jade handle. All these details configured a fragile and vulnerable woman, but her psychic energy and intuitive powers revealed otherwise.

One day while waiting for a streetlight to change in San Francisco, a young man came up behind Frida and offered his arm to assist her in crossing the busy San Francisco Mission intersection. As they walked arm in arm, she immediately became alert to danger. She turned her face fully to the young man and, gazing deeply into his eyes, asked, *"How can I help you, dear man?"* He looked stunned and backed up, as though being stripped of all his clothing, and began to weep. They did not exchange words; she rather just gazed upon him for a long moment in silence with great love and offered him one of the many pens she carried in her oversized purse to take down her phone number. She invited him to come and see her at her home for a session. He scribbled it on the palm of his hand and quickly ran away without looking back.

After a few weeks he called her, and she invited him to see her at her apartment in the Mission district in San Francisco. They began to talk, and he confessed his intentions that day on the street. He said he was going to rob her and steal her purse, but her candid gaze took him by such surprise, he could not do it. He confessed he cried for weeks. He said that he could see her eyes for days and this experience caused him to see something greater in himself that he had never before seen. He knew he was a good man but something in himself was pushing him toward reprehensible behavior such as robbery from elders. Something in her eyes validated his true nature. She confirmed this in their following sessions, which she offered to work with him without any financial exchange. He began to work for her doing odd jobs and secretarial help and became a devoted student. His success in his professional life as a doctor was confirmed in later years. Frida truly believed as the old Jewish proverb prescribes, *"If you help one person, you help the whole world."*

Hundreds of people came through Frida's door every year either by acquaintance or accident, such as the young man who wanted to rob her. She met each person authentically one at a time, sometimes walking on the street, in counsel in her apartment, or sometimes for tea. She formed women's and men's groups to study and work on collective issues arising from gender profiling, violence, addictions, parental abuse, relationship distress, children's problems, projections, fear, and spiritual confusion, such as obedience to dominant authority figures. She taught all students how to apply the Three Selves method to all these issues and no matter how badly she was feeling, never missed a scheduled class.

It is said in the ancient writings of the Sufi mystics that a wise person can arouse people to confess the secrets of their hearts, hidden thoughts, and feelings, which have made them ill in some way. Frida could read others decisively and when anyone visited her in her quarters, she always said, *"They had to leave their garbage outside,"* in order to feel the generosity of a truly insightful master by coming before a being who was a superb dedicated instrument of the Most High. She was willing to accept them and willing to listen to what is arising and unknown.

Participatory Synchronicity

I dreamed of Frida 12 years prior to meeting her. When I arrived in San Francisco, I was living in a Sufi Islamia Ruhaniat Khankah (presently called Sufi Ruhaniat International), a collective dwelling of disciples, The Garden of Shafayat, with a masterful Hakim (healer), Murshid Saul-uddin Barodofsky, studying the methods of healing transmission from the Sufi Message work of Hazrat Inayat Khan, who brought the Sufi Message of Spiritual Liberty to the West. Murshid Saul-uddin indicated that a special guest was coming for dinner that night and we all went into overdrive to put together a full course dinner for the occasion. When the doorbell rang, I answered it and to my surprise there was the woman in my dream standing before me. Her poignant words, *"Well, it took you long enough to get here, I have been waiting for you for many years."* At that moment, I knew when I met Frida, it was a destined meeting based on my earlier dream. Although I did not understand the prophetic nature of the dream at the time, I soon came to understand how participatory synchronicity is an aspect that each person innately is given as a beneficent gift of awakening consciousness.

In my dream, I was in a large rectangular barn, and at the other end, opposite to me, was this small, white-haired woman with glasses. She beckoned to me to come to her not by any motion of her hands but rather through her silent intention. She pulled me toward her in the same way as two magnets might draw together. We moved closer to each other but our feet did not move. As I stood in front of her and opened both my hands, palms upward as though in a respectful mudra of openness and receptivity, within an instant, in my right hand appeared the image of a perfect holographic male person but in miniature. In my left hand appeared a perfect holographic female person in miniature. I stood amazed at these images as they were living. When I gazed back into her eyes again, she pulled out a long silver needle. It glistened in the light and then she thrust it into the center crown at the top of my skull driving it down my spine to my coccyx bone. This action turned everything into white light and caused a tremendous amount of pain, which woke me up out of the dream state screaming. My perception was radically shifted that day after the dream. Everything in my life, as I knew it, changed from that point on.

Twelve years later to the day, the doorbell rang at the Garden of Shafayat and as I opened the door my life changed again. Joyfully and with great gratitude, a profound relationship developed with Frida over the amazing 15 years that I worked spiritually with her until the day she died on November 18, 1989.

Her committed approach was unique. She began to tell me the story of her rape as a child. Her story detailed pain, fear, and self-diminishment—all the feelings that can surface in any woman for different reasons. It seemed she was talking about the universal state of women's vulnerability and the suffering they experienced in societies that do not take action against systemic forms of brutality accepted so casually in patriarchal cultures around the globe. The absence of her parents' protection, the poverty during the Depression era, and many other conditions found in her narrative compiled the data for her sharing. She, too, had a connective awareness with women who experience the same kind of marginalization by unconscious domination strategies.

She insisted I listen carefully to her words and not project onto my own story. Her sharing eventually derailed my conceptual frame because as she began to speak, I began to access a bridge to myself that was structured by Frida's spiritual transformation. She began to detail the reasons behind the experiences that propelled her Divine plan forward. I was beginning to sense qualities of *"participatory synchronicity"* with her life experiences joining with my life experiences. I could understand the suffering of her muted and suppressed child and her desire to speak out against the person who raped her. Her difficulty to balance these painful memories, and how these feelings identified a genuine framework of sustained oppression in the lives of women, became powerfully translucent. As Frida brought to my awareness the larger endemic problem for women in society, she offered her transmission of balance between the male and female basic selves within each one of us to emphasize how women's transformative consciousness needs to take place in order for the domination paradigm to change. For the evolution of consciousness can truly arise through those who are the instruments of those painful sufferings as they are not victims but ministers of transformation for all of humanity. Doing her own inner work, she mapped out the Three Selves method that opened understanding to her karmic patterns. She felt that each woman must do their own work by asking and seeking out their Higher Purpose which will not only transform themselves but most surely affect the greater collective and this can occur by accessing one's High Self. She did the same for all men who sought her wisdom as well. As Mahatma Gandhi said, *"Change yourself, you change the world."*

The Three Selves method, which balances the basic selves with the High Self, unraveled the tangled knots of awareness in my own psyche because of her constant encouragement to listen and come back into full presence to her story, her energy, her wisdom, and her use of a loving transmission to detail how the basic selves were developing their ability to abide or resist their High Self wisdom. As I applied an "imitation technique" it became a helpful primary method for understanding a non-attached approach to becoming more present and mindful with my state of being. It was difficult at first because the mind-mesh leaks memories into consciousness and one travels into these thoughts as though in a momentary haze instead of being present with what needs to be learned in the moment. Her study groups held a simple principle: we had to listen carefully with full presence to each other's story and then listen to how we are using the information to learn about ourselves. It was a true method that reflected "pairing" (seeing the world that is within me from another's eyes). This technique became the learning ground for applying Fourth Wave Feminine Principles.

But the manner of her intuitive insight, which illuminated Frida's story, was the way she listened to her inner High Self, conscious self, and basic selves that led her to essential seeing what she called "*spiritual insight*" when she was blind. It was during this period that she grasped the inner details of her childhood rape. Her sense of loss of control, the pain and the pleasure, all confused in a child's mind, correlated to feelings in my emotional body about being unconscious of who I was as a woman. All the paradoxical feelings that I had experienced within myself were given "*co-presence*" (mutual participation) with another living being, Frida. I did not only feel confirmed about my ability to read what was going on in my body, but rather I felt united with the human species. Women and men have all been mothers at one time in their evolution and the Divine Holy Mother-Gaia unfolds the seeds of these memories that build connection and empathy. It was an amazing universal knowing, a validation of sorts, that acknowledged a feminist epistemology, the woman's body as a source of Sacred Wisdom.

Frida's philosophy when using the Three Selves method was explained in the way she understood "control" and how this concept is often misunderstood in the West whose manner of understanding control is via domination of a stronger over a weaker participant. But Frida related her experience of the meaning of control as a concentration developed from esoteric principles. She related control to surrender to the Divine Will through the High Self. She indicated this idea did not mean surrendering to a person, per se, but rather how, through any relationship, we can learn vulnerability and therefore develop an awareness of a greater surrender with what she called "*a finite being.*" If we have no control of the growth of our hair and nails, our birth and our death, we should not assume we could control the things that happen to us. Any learning experience that arises in our lifetime is a gradual process from overt to more subtle nuances. It takes great courage to totally release our human will to Divine Will because it is a radical way of living by respecting the complex shape our lives take. Being aware in this manner is a form of learning unconditional receptivity while remaining actively generous in our reciprocal actions. She conveyed how our human desires grow less important as we begin to understand the value of listening and acting from our inner sensing that arises from a deeper connection with our inner life. How important our bodies are as instruments of this kind of knowledge, especially if we begin to view our bodies as spiritual instruments: this was an important contemplation.

I realized during our working sessions how vital it was to connect psychically to the global community of women. In doing so, great strength and insight is given to any individual woman because it is the inner reality of women who make the spiritual world

62

knowable through their bodies, which create life. To listen and act on the information our bodies are giving us takes courage to stand against those that would mute and misuse the body's essence and purpose. From my vantage point, I knew what needed to happen, and I needed to believe I could take the responsibility to awaken and listen deeply to what was somatically congruent with my intuition. It would be a mistake today to not recognize the risk as well as the sociological paradigm that sets women up not to follow what they know from within their own bodies. But cautionary warning seems to guide actions that following intuition. The foundation for action has to stand on ethical ground that upholds women's respectful regard for their bodies first and foremost, and this should be the beginning from where the highest level of moral law begins. When we are respectful to our bodies as women and men, we become exemplars of the Sacred Feminine within all actions and then the Divine Mother of the World-Gaia is there with us, as we will do the same for Her. When misguided actions go against the beneficial principles that can protect women, anything sociologically compromising the intuitive and somatic well-being, women must realign to the essential arising awareness that their bodies are sacred instruments of the Divine Holy Mother. That essential awareness of Her Presence within will inform them as to whether they should concur with an action or reject it.

If women wish to become free of dominant paradigms that keep them chained to actions that negate their body's sense of knowing, then the price will be even greater later as awareness is a living spiritual presence of the Great Holy Mother-Gaia's selfhood. Although she has witnessed the holocaust of Her Own Being, She patiently forges through the present dominant perceptions that marginalize, infantilize, and position women in subservience that do not reflect the Divine Mother's true being. It is the individual women who deeply trust their bodies' somatic knowing and who speaks from that place, who will change the sociological paradigm. Annette Baier, a cultural ethicist, says, *"Yet if I am right in claiming that morality, as anything more than a law within itself requires trust in order to thrive, and that immorality too thrives on some form of trust, it seems obvious that we ought...to look into the question of what forms of trust are needed for the thriving of the version of morality we endorse, and into the morality of that and other forms of trust."* [xxix]

The virtue of trust necessitates a right to be heard. Baier further shows how the power to use language to speak out about women's rights is necessary, she says, *"The power thus externalized and objectivized are our individual powers to participate in and benefit from cooperative practices, and most fundamentally in speech. If there is any basic right, it is the right to be heard, to participate in normative discussion. One's first claim is the claim to voice, to one's turn to speak and to be listened to."* [xxx]

Frida maintained her spiritual practice and her right to speak out what she experienced from the inner reality of her Three Selves method. Her intuitive skills were an example to all who knew her and worked with her. She voiced her wisdom born from her inner selves to many who even rejected her because they were not ready to hear the voice of truth that they themselves had articulated and who did not yet believe in who they were. She always said she was the *"Gadfly"* in the room, who persistently stimulated psychic connections with the inner selves of those she worked with, sometimes causing criticism of her work when people were not ready to take on the changes that were necessary for their spiritual growth.

Her death was a testament to the conscious awakened and integrated High Self, conscious self, and basic selves. Three days prior to her last breath, she was working

64

with her Female Basic Self, who she called, *"Binky."* Frida had to prepare Binky to let go of the body and follow the High Self into separation from the body. Binky didn't like this news that transformation was afoot and was very rebellious, giving argument to Frida that she still wanted to hang around in the physical form. Frida had to tell Binky about death as a non-ending but rather a continuation only in another non-material form for a period of time until the cycle would recur, if necessary. This helped Binky become more tranquil but something happened three days before Frida died that made the Three Selves method a reality to my conscious perception.

Frida was lying on the daybed in the living room during the nine-month period of her transition, and I was sleeping in the same room only a little distance away from her on the soft-carpeted floor so that I would be close to her in case she needed me. I was her major caretaker even though I had organized a group of dedicated women to care for her during this period. I was on duty this night. It was dawn when I heard Frida's soft moaning. I woke from a light sleep and saw in the Eastern window the figure of a beautiful, thin, young woman, in a red and white silk polka-dot dress, wearing a small black hat and high heels with ankle straps, and nylon stockings that women wore in the 1920s with a seam up the back of the leg. She was smoking a cigarette and pulling on drags of smoke. Her demeanor was quite agitated and one could tell by the way she was smoking the cigarette that she was annoyed, jerking her hand from her mouth to the air like a Joan Crawford characterization. I thought I was dreaming and wondered how this person entered into the room without me hearing the doorbell. I rubbed my eyes and shook my head from my sleepiness and when I looked up again, she was gone. Frida moaned a bit at that moment and I went to her. I asked her if she needed anything. Frida said Binky was having a hard time and she didn't like the destination plan. I described the woman I had seen standing in the window, and Frida said, "Yes I know, that is Binky, she loves red and white polka-dot dresses but I have to work with her until she arrives at acceptance, otherwise I will be hanging here in this old body." It took Frida three days to finalize her agreements with Binky and then Frida made her transition.

It was not until that moment that I realized the power of Three Selves method that Frida introduced into the Western psycho-spiritual consciousness and how these entities of our collaborative incarnation are genuine aspects of our composite self. Frida's respect and consideration for their working agreements with High Self, conscious self, and basic selves have been an invaluable tool kit for people who wish to advance toward their awakening process and into their soul's purpose while honoring their unique development into Feminine Fourth Wave development.

Of all the experiences I had the privilege of learning was the exchange Frida and I had together in the bond that knew we would always be together in many lifetimes, bringing each other into remembrance of our Higher Purpose as we shared being a guide and teacher to one another in different lifetimes. This was well understood in our inner work and we honored each other as catalysts for Divine Remembrance. These are my experiences and absorption of Frida and her Three Self teachings. What comes forward in your consciousness when you read these experiences?

How Different Approaches in Psychology Alter Our Perception

The different approaches found in psychology that alter our perception have always been a topic of great interest to me. It might appear an odd juncture to leap into different aspects of these approaches at this point in the middle of this book, but perhaps the reader might wish to investigate the reasons motivating this choice. The main reason concerns the verbalization of meaning and language. Some male scholars, whose methods are reflective of the theophany found in spiritual exegesis such as in mystical Sufism or Christianity, express clear and integrative pathways to find the Self within. (These scholars will be mentioned in the text below). Their methods reveal the seed impetus of how the Holy Mother of the World-Gaia furthers unifying investigation into co-presence, consilience, pairing, and participatory synchronicity bringing Fourth Wave Feminine Principles to the forefront. When I contemplate the hagiographic material of these Holy Women, it is evident how transcendental phenomenology, for example, offers a viable structure for connecting the inner and outer aspects of a narrative to any reader's psychological experiences. Within Fourth Wave Feminine Principles, although sometimes varied, it advocates proximity of inner motivation to social action [xxxi] such as found in the experiences of Mother Teresa, Noor-un-nisa Inayat Khan, and Reverend Frida Waterhouse. Together their approaches take into account women's intuitive feelings, their spiritual quest, their personal view of the world and themselves, their private concepts, their strivings for self-actualization, and their contribution to social justice. As their lives correlate with my own life experiences, one can sense how transcendental phenomenology coheres well with hermeneutical and Fourth Wave Feminine Principles because the approaches fulfill the function that is accomplished in bridging psychological information into conscious action. Although these might simply be research terms to some readers, it seems to me that women's spiritual hagiographic material, whatever richness our own experiences offer, can induce greater and expanded realization of sacred principles that alter our perception of ourselves and the world.

The intriguing correlation of Holy Women who lived in the past and the uniting of the same phenomena that emerge in my own consciousness actualize for me the inherent alchemy found in great souls that identify the humblest aspects of human intuitive experience as an intimate and mysterious meeting ground of consideration for all of us. Edmond Husserl (1977) defined the term *co-presence* as *"the other and I would be the same."* [xxxii] I found Husserl's words distinctively true when working with both Mother Teresa and Reverend Frida Waterhouse.

The sense of co-presence is most exquisitely presented in the following words of Simone Weil (1909-1943): *"The world is the closed door. It is a barrier. And at the same time it is a way through. Two prisoners whose cells adjoin communicate with each other by knocking on the wall. The wall is the thing that separates them but it is also their means of communication... every separation is a link."* [xxxiii] We know from phenomenological observation, as Ulrich Neisser stated, *"Whether beautiful or ugly or just conveniently at hand, the world of experience is produced by the [woman], who experiences it."* [xxxiv] Neisser suggested a potential and unique insight into the "complexified" [xxxv] world of meaning that Jean Gebser stated could give evidence to a unique integration of sacred transmission. Reading the experiences of wise beings

68

and/or spending time with Holy Women in real life brings testament to the One Life behind the individual life repeating itself at each birth and each identity. If we desire spiritual messages from the Holy Mother of the World-Gaia, we will receive them from someone somewhere because they are in us already as we are part of them. I give attention to the values and uniqueness of each of these Eight Holy Women's experiences, because I attempt to absorb the impulse through somatic knowing and intuition showing what lived at the core of each persona and in me.

My story functions as an indication of mutual participation through arising sympathetic awareness in and to the soul that has become utterly transparent to the Holy Mother's Being. My being only makes herself known to the exalted counterpart who was once exiled through my own ignorance and is given a welcomed return to a fully transcendental existence.

As I approached this process, the hagiographies uniquely reveal a quadrant of inter-subjective ways of bringing spiritual evidence forward about our intuitive processes found through the four qualitative criteria defined below: transcendental, pairing, co-presence, and consilience. To guide the reader, I introduce these four criteria for enhancing levels of application toward one's own psycho-spiritual process.

Transcendental Awareness

Although the term "transcendental" might be assumed to mean going beyond one's experience, these two male writers, M. Farber [xxxvi] and C. Moustakas, [xxxvii] listed meanings that they found would reveal a new definition of the term. For example, *"Transcendental"* begins with the things of life themselves. The Holy Women's hagiographic material is not concerned with matters of fact but rather it seeks to determine meaning found in their experiences and looks into essence and possible essences. How self-giving brings insight to oneself and others and how does the Holy Woman obtain insight through the state of pure subjectivity, while reflecting on the Divine Source of all Creation when engaging with life experiences.

A natural question arises concerning the validity of what we see, feel, and sense and which might indeed be misunderstood as a fiction. One person might experience one thing while reading a hagiographic account, and another person might find something else, but as the stories unfold and my story becomes intertwined with these Holy Women, what might be apprehended by yet another reader is a transcendental "fresh" way of knowing many complex systems of interpretation. One or more of these millions of sensory stimuli could illuminate a sense of connection sparking intuition and opening yet another deeper meaning in how these Holy Women, the Great Mother of the

World-Gaia, and the reader might interface in a real-time, living theophany, a unity awareness, and synchronicity. This benefits all beings by bringing a generous and exponential gift of seeding awareness from the Divine Mother of the World-Gaia to all involved. This is a true example of how Fourth Wave Feminism works.

Pairing

Members of the psychological profession have spent years focusing on understanding how an individual perceives, synthesizes, and interprets feelings, one's worldview, one's inner life, and the nature of subjective sensing. Writers like William James [xxxviii]; Rogers, [xxxix]; Moustakas, [xl]and Creswell [xli] all describe multiplicities of experience that align with the idea of *"pairing."* Pairing is seeing the world that is within me from another's eyes. This term encourages us to look at the interrelated components that primarily form a communion of spirit and evaluate it to a dimension where another's experience informs my own, cognitively and experientially.

There are obvious limitations that should be considered at this point. Holy Women who are historical figures, such as Mother Teresa, Noor-un-nisa Inayat Khan, and Reverend Amanuensis Frida Waterhouse, are no longer living. The inter-subjective communication between persons who translate their understanding of someone else in order to understand themself is one-sided. Another limitation found in hagiographic data collected from secondary literary sources such as biographical or ethnographic material can include inferences from writers and not necessarily reflect the historic person's true sense of being. As the Holy Women are not living to validate elements of their experience, a Fourth Wave Feminine Principle offers a suggestion for the integration of these variables.

Sometimes rereading patiently of a Holy Woman's life story is recommended, especially when the reader realizes the same recurring description which evokes an "*innate knowing*," and is perceived with respect to the intention of discovering something within one's psyche that is trying to reveal itself. The reader then eliminates redundancies and begins to perceive connective meaning-units. Meaning-units bring together spiritual pairing lines between two Holy Women, the historic person, and the present-day person reading the hagiology. It is similar to what Simone Weil says: *"In order to come to us God passes through the infinite thickness of time and space; (her) grace changes nothing in the play of those blind forces of necessity and change that guides the world; it penetrates into our souls as a drop of water makes its way through geological strata without affecting their structure, and there it waits in silence until we consent to become God again."* [xlii]

Through Fourth Wave Feminine Principles, similar meaning-units might occur, but they would be assembled through the integration of the distance between the reader and the sources of stimuli about the Holy Woman's life. This is understood by regarding the proximity and correlation of phenomena instead. This is done through the aspect of co-presence.

Co-Presence

To enhance clear observation of self we find the need to acknowledge the biases that can exist, through what may be termed in Fourth Wave Feminine Principles as an intuitive experience or a *co-presence* with another body of information coexisting with

my body of intuitive experience. [xliii] A communion arises in the reader who is directly

present to a description as defined in the Latin *"communionem,"* meaning *"mutual*

participation." The idea introduces the reader to the task of identifying the

phenomenon of an intuitional experience and correlating it to the same intuitional

experience living within the reader. This will bring about the aspect of consilience.

Consilience

This type of synchronistic correlation can be understood as a concept of

consilience. This term was coined by the British polymath (philosopher of science),

William Whewell (1794-1866). [xliv] Whewell's *"consilience of induction"* occurred when

an induction obtained from one class of facts coincided with an induction obtained from

a different class of facts. This consilience was one of several tests of validity of the theory

in which it occurred. Consilience means, literally, *"to leap with"* or *"to jump together."*

In an explanatory surprise, two or more sets of inductions jump together and are seen to

be importantly interrelated. [xlv] Using Whewell's idea, the reader and the Holy Woman

can obtain a framework that explicates their experiences from various descriptions

while addressing ours in a mutual situation and historic timeframe.

The concept of consilience elucidates Fourth Wave Feminine Principles to

transcendental phenomenology and hermeneutic studies. By its inherent meaning,

consilience can link these great and Holy Women's contributions to religious thought

and post-modern philosophy by bringing new relevance to stereotypic concepts that

inform women's social behavior, particularly during times of historic isolation, oppression, and physical incapacity such as during World War II, the Depression, and societal class separation, religious stigmatization in the ongoing centuries, and so on. The same correlation can bring fresh meaning to how spiritual codes of behavior and intuitive understanding of these codes can inspire individuals to take altruistic actions. If we grasp what Simone Weil indicates when she says: *"The only organ of contact with existence is acceptance, love"*. That is why beauty and reality are solace to the soul. That is why joy and the sense of reality are identical of the same light source. *(l'amour n'est pas consolation, il est lumière.)* [xlvi]

The stories of Mother Teresa, Noor-un-nisa Inayat Khan, and Reverend Amanuensis Frida Waterhouse can inspire in us new epistemologies for learning how to read ourselves as women who strive for social autonomy and spiritual unity based on sacred relationships with the Holy Mother of the World-Gaia, with ourselves, and with all beings who are essentially One Being. The use of consilience brings evidence to how experiences far and near *"jump together,"* offering substantive connections never before dreamed.

Merleau Ponty (1962) pointed out how the real essence of essence is not to be constructed or explained. This is the appeal to one who uses narrative material to prepare oneself for expanded ways of knowing that can bring to life universal expressions that unite us in a more fulfilled human condition. Social psychologists have recognized the need to see greater influence of interpersonal relations and group membership through investigation of attitudes within group dynamics. The emergence of the roles of personality on group dynamics has given rise to information that shows how particular prophetic roles become important as they not only serve to integrate the individual but also effect the primary group and the collective behavior of the greater

74

community. The best examples of this can be found in hagiographic material referred to in this book.

However, when a reader experiences a living person a similar understanding abides, as A. Giorgi (1985) cautioned us to be aware, *"that a human subject is also historical and social and dwells in a world of meanings."* [xlvii] Whether or not we hermeneutically dig down into a hagiography or collect data from a living person, the idea of Whewell's consilience is worthy to ponder. Whewell's idea is edified by Abraham Maslow (1965) who said, *"Every person is, in part, [her] own project, and makes [herself]."* [xlviii] His assertion indicates how an individual is encouraged to use individual volition and then places themselves in relation to a group and the group then arranges to the individual. This is evident in the relationship Mother Teresa had with the Catholic Church, Reverend Amanuensis Waterhouse with her Jewish traditional faith, and Noor-un-nisa Khan to the Sufi mystical training from her father, Hazrat Inayat Khan.

As a person searching for meaning explores the arising experiences of their development, every investigation and exploration matures the spirit by developing a unified sense of selfhood, and this means experiencing the world more as a reflection of one's own nature and one's own nature as the world. Correlation produces a valid awareness of one's self as the enlargement of self is dependent upon and in turn supports the breadth of world community and its values.

Our intuitive experiences can reveal hidden categories and codes that determine an inner exegesis—a unity awareness that rejects subject/object valuing alone. Combined and respecting Fourth Wave Feminine Principles, every person can ride out the flow of intuitive *"leaping together"* of experiences and arrive at a new spiritual realm where the ego self leaves and only the Holy Mother of the World-Gaia exists. This type of spiritual synthesis can also be achieved when the past phenomena of historic individuals are found operating in the person's present-time psycho-spiritual momentum. Fourth Wave Feminine Principles is committed to exploration in these four areas of the 1) the transcendental, 2) pairing, 3) co-presence, and 4) consilience. The phenomena that became operative in my life consisted of the Holy Women's internal intuitive development that arose in me while contemplating these Holy Women's hagiographies.

The intuitive phenomena uniting these hagiographies and us are based on alignment of faith, the inner integrity of their course of action in the world. The doubtlessness that arose in these Holy Women when faced with limitations within religious laws, domination strategies, marginalization, proto-typing or threat of bodily harm makes them true leaders. We are faced with the question, did these Holy Women succeed? Did their life story clarify anything for us in our reflection on our spiritual path and our soul's unfoldment? Did the defining choice to live from one's intuitive knowing while forging ahead against oppressive proto-typing becomes a beacon to their spiritual evolution?

Fourth Wave Feminine Principles considers these questions because the synchronicity of the entirety of the experience of one's life is sacred.

> *"If I look at my whole stock of your lived experiences and ask about the structure of this knowledge, one thing becomes clear: This is that everything I know about your conscious life is really based on my knowledge of my own lived experiences. My lived experiences of you are constituted in simultaneity or quasi-simultaneity with your lived experiences, to which they are intentionally*

related. It is only because of this that, when I look backward, I am able to synchronize my past experiences of you with your past experiences." [xlix]

The four approaches for psychological self-examination: transcendental, pairing, co-presence, and consilience as examination of one's intuitive nature deepens through correlating phenomena linking to my experiences. They emerge up through a reduced attitude, meaning... I sought out the essence of each phenomenon through the application of free imaginative variations while respecting the fact that my conscious choices reflect the sum total of themselves by grouping the sum structural essences of the Holy Women's experiences. As William James (1892, 1961, 2001) indicated, and I paraphrase, it is not only a person's body and psychic powers but in the widest possible sense, a person's understanding of what is "me" becomes the sum total of all that she can call hers. I found connection with these Holy Women's experiences as they searched for themselves as representatives of the Holy Mother of the World-Gaia. How I sustained connection with these Holy Women's hagiographies was based on the following observations.

Self-Observation from Inner Judgment

Within the acknowledgment of one's inner judgment is the freedom from inner judgment. It is the same if one accepts a criticism; one frees oneself of the criticism. As long as judgment is acknowledged, we confirm the validity of our experiences with the individual hagiographies, and in this study, the Fourth Wave Feminine Principles, self-examination is expected. What Holy Women face universally as oppressive socialization is a running theme in this study but there is more revealed in the inner and mystical aspects of experiences that will be dealt with in the next Chapter II, that references, Mary Baker Eddy, Julian of Norwich, Hazrat Babajan, Sanapia, and Dr. Rina Sircar.

Our unique awareness of one's own historic timeframe and any form of oppression that we experience as women requires that we remain astute to our inner judgment while absorbing through the Holy Women's experiences what these differences bring to our felt-sense. The *"leaping together"* of accumulated information, and suggested feminine intuitive approaches to interpreting experiences as stated above, gather evidence of a valid, collective, *"social experience of women."*[1] The correlation of my lived experiences with the Holy Women's hagiographies may bring forward inherent judgments that can arise in how I interpret what they went through. Judgments are acceptable as long as they are stated. Judgments give us the opportunity to open up unexamined concepts that might bring illumination to the limited capacity of our intuition and expand our consciousness to the ancient formulas still living in social behavior or passed down as familial paradigms that prevent self-awareness from arising.

Self-Observation Leading Back to the Source of Meaning

Self-observation begins with openness to the boundaries between the person being studied and the psychological condition of the person who, as a united observer, is exploring the source of meaning. There is no prejudgment of what is being stated and observed. Open observation between the time/space abstractions among generations could reveal an existing experiential link as the physical/psychic world remains in a permeable involvement. This criterion addresses how a unified reduction described in

Fourth Wave Feminine principles removes the observational dualism of EMIC/ETIC stances (stories than can be observed as an insider or outsider to the community ethos). (The EMIC/ETIC stances were coined by Kenneth Pike [1967] as a linguistic perspective that can be applied to any sociological or cultural system.) EMIC comes from the word "*phonemic*" which means language that is common to the native speaker, and ETIC means "*phonetic*" and relies upon the extrinsic concepts and categories of language. [li]

The EMIC/ETIC categories can assist observation because the transcendent process makes known the inter-subjective perceptions of what is real and unites both internal and external observational realities by enhancing reduction of what differentiates. [lii] Reduction, in this sense, directs us back to the source of unification with the Holy Mother of the World-Gaia, the one who is searching, in this case, which is absorbing the meaning and existence of the experienced world of the Holy Women in and through themselves.

Self-Observation of Essence through Respectful Partnerships

Acknowledging the lived experience of the Holy Woman who dedicated her life to repairing social inequity and bringing forward the spiritual pairing of the celestial counterpart of each one of us, requires a prudent person to deliberate well about what is good or expedient for oneself, not with a view for some particular end such as recognition or gaining power over others, a dominant paradigm that is ethically disrespectful and destructive, but rather for the purpose of living a fully awakened life.

Therefore, the reader's respect toward an individual's spiritual and dedicated life encapsulates the initial approach to the study of the Holy Woman in this text. Then the reader can approach the search for essence through the artful idea of bringing something descriptive into being, this is an ancient idea brought into realization by Aristotle: *"And every art is concerned with bringing something into being, i.e., with contriving or calculating how to bring into being some one of those things that can either be or not be, and the cause of whose production lies in the producer, not in the thing itself which is produced. For art has not to do with that which is or comes into being of necessity, nor with the products of nature; for these have the cause of their production in themselves."* [liii] The multiple patterns arising from the various narratives correlated to the experiences of the one who is searching can shape the ethical attitudes of the inquiry. The search for essence and one's ethical motivation to remain consistently engaged with oneself and one's inner intuitive sense builds the respect for cooperative partnerships within a spiritual context of ego self and higher self-knowing.

Observation of Intentionality and Connection as Values Leap Together

Remaining present to our feelings through an *"intuitive-sense"* arising through consilience, pairing, and correlation are primary practices for understanding Fourth Wave Feminine Principles as it opens a connection to others. Values of a reader become integrated into the observational process when experiences from a specific Holy Woman's hagiography *"leap together"* bringing about consilience, and form a sympathetic resonance that ultimately influences another way of negotiating the structure of reality for the reader that has not been known before in the evolving story of the reader's journey and can be rediscovered, as Husserl indicated, through the real event that can only be discovered by being lived. Bergson (1946) verified this idea by calling things that cannot be grasped through immobile concepts but only through intuitional sensitivity can a person be guided, inspired, and protected. [liv]"In principle, Moustakas agrees, *"there is within me a realm of virtually infinite access to other human beings."* [lv]

The core and nucleus of our self-knowing is the very sanctuary of our life; it is the sense of activity which certain inner states possess. This *"sense of activity"* is often held to be a direct revelation of the living substance of our Soul. [lvi] The Holy Women referenced in this text, their cultures, ages, religious devotions, abilities, and intuitive understandings provide insight for the reader's unique spiritual awakening as well as offering practical ways of addressing reality in the moment as it did for me, the ninth woman in this study.

Differences need not be seen as distractions but rather as forces awakening the Creative Mover, the Holy Mother of the World-Gaia, who is behind the unique heart of individuation. As the reader reads the stories of these Holy Women, soul and Creature draw closer together, maintaining care for this precious communion in an arising integral synthesis. The intuitive ways of knowing within the context of how we experience ourselves captivates the moment and will be the determining force of the reader's fate.

Qualities of the Mother of the World-Gaia

The Holy Mother of the World-Gaia is reflected through all of these Holy Women's actions listed and running through this text. In the second section of this manuscript, I give evidence as to how the Mother of the World-Gaia lives through Her chosen representative revealing Her Divine Essence through vision and intuitive action. As evidenced in the next series of Holy Women, the Holy Mother of the World offers help to people in need; She counsels those who seek wisdom, truth, and happiness; She reaches into the fog of forgotten ideals of the soul on its journey though the many forms and guides them safely to their spiritual home; She brings realization and connection to an ever-living affirmation of trust in the body as a form of knowledge and to the continuum of creative soulfulness with all relations; She offers the rainbow arc of justice sometimes through the actions of willing self-sacrifice for others; She counters hatred, intolerance, and ruthlessness found in old dominant paradigms that are anathema to her sense of beauty, balance, and compassion; She shatters philosophical dualisms with integral awareness between body, mind, and spirit that forge spiritual cohesion between both genders—female and male.

She is the essence of the universal form of Love. As Mother Mirra Alfassa says, "*O Mother universal, and in this double identity with That which is beyond and That which is all the manifestation they taste the infinite joy of the perfect certitude....Mother, sweet Mother who I am, Thou art at once the destroyer and the builder. The whole universe lives in Thy breast with all its life innumerable and Thou livest in Thy immensity in the least of its atoms. And the aspiration of Thy infinitude turn towards that which is not manifested to cry to it for a manifestation ever more complete and more perfect. All is, in one time, in a triple and clairvoyant total Consciousness, the Individual, the Universal, the Infinite".* [lvii]

She is the essence of perfect archetypal balance between male and female because she takes the higher, holier consciousness of spirit and finds it in all things that are gender differentiated and yet united. Julian of Norwich synthesizes this idea perfectly by experiencing Jesus through the feminine: *"So Jesus Christ who sets good against evil is our real Mother. We owe our being to him, and this is the essence of motherhood, and all the delightful, loving protection which ever follows. God is as really our Mother as our Father...The human mother will suckle her child with her own milk, but our beloved Mother, Jesus, feeds us with himself, and, with the most tender of courtesy, does it by means of the blessed Sacrament, the precious food of all true life."* [lviii]

Only through the cherishing of wisdom through beauty, balance, and experiences that honor compassion of both female and male congruence can happiness essentially be found. Great thinkers of the ancient world declared that happiness does not come from fame or fortune but rather the mind that is wise finds the lasting satisfaction. It is the desire for experiencing wisdom that is the key needed to open the intuitional door to liberation. It is interesting that Roger Bacon (1266-1268) calls the talent of intuition closely to the mind quality of the Great Mother of the World-Gaia when he says, *"For there are two modes of acquiring knowledge, namely by reasoning and experience.*

Reasoning draws a conclusion and makes us grant the conclusion, but does not make the conclusion certain, nor does it remove doubt so that the mind can rest on the intuition of truth unless the mind discovers it by the path of experience." [lix] It is experience that is the key that links the Holy Women to me and to the readers of this book.

The Mind Factor

There is great unanimity among the ancient patriarchal philosophers and the Holy Women explored in the following pages of this text as they provide a window into the values of the mind as a pathway to accomplishment. That pathway is built into the unified vision of the Holy Mother of the World-Gaia, the *"philosophia eternus"* not as a pantheistic idea but one as training the mind to understand the Divine in all that is living. One can understand this important point through the many dedicated contributions of the next series of Prophetic Women who illuminated the world with their minds, hearts, and souls.

Mary Baker Eddy, who is a leading Prophet of the Christian Science Church and a proponent of the Science of Mind, indicates, *"In Science, Mind is one, including noumenon and phenomena, God and thoughts. Mortal mind is a solecism in language, and involves an improper use of the word mind. As Mind is immortal, the phrase mortal mind implies something untrue and therefore unreal; and as the phrase is used in teaching Christian Science, it is meant to designate that which has no real existence."* [lx] She illuminates this idea further in the dedicated sections that follow.

From the Buddhist Meditation Master, Dr. Rina Sircar says, *"Developing calmness through meditation is the practice which tranquilizes and humbles the mind, making it clearer and brighter, until it is empty and radiant. In this way, a new mind is uncovered, a "right mind" which is powerfully simple, creatively silent, energetically still."* lxi

The development of mental powers aligning with a spiritual power is exemplified in the healing work of Sanapia, Eagle Doctor of the Comanche people. Although never educated in the English language, she declares in her unique manner the connection to spirit and mind that inspired her healing methods. She says, *"The eagle got more power than anything living, I guess, it got Medicine to help people get well...to cure them. I got power like that eagle because the eagle help me when I call on it when I doctor. My mother told me that I be just like that eagle when I doctor. I can feel the eagle working in me when I doctor and try hard to get someone well. Feels like that eagle tell me in my mind to go ahead and fix that person up...get him well."* lxii

Various scholars have studied and written about the lives of these women and how they understood the mind as they followed their various religious callings. It is a joy and a privilege to walk in time with these particular representatives of spiritual and visionary perception because they were motivated toward caring for the Holy Mother-Gaia's creation by following their spiritual and mental stream of unique discipline and intuitional calling. The various religious paradigms from which these Holy Women were formed sets the framework of their inherent struggles as women in male-dominated religious leadership that focused more on power and control and claims that the Divine

Source is male rather than using the mind to relieve human suffering. The sociological repression arising in their historic timeframe is daunting to say the least. Bringing through their spiritual contribution to the world under such limitation helps the reader understand true Fourth Wave Feminine epistemology of transformation. Their level of transformation break away from the dominant paradigms such as doctrinal control, gender-specific limitations, and cultural deviations that ignorantly wanted to disempower women as lower than the Divine Creator by attempting to control the outer means of the adept. The dominant paradigm is a self-destructing system for this very reason and offers a strategy that will never work. Helpless and unable to limit the super-celestial soul and the reason why the Holy Mother of the World-Gaia appears in any timeframe and in any individual that seeks the Creation's benefit, the dominant paradigm becomes obsolete.

There is a sacred current arising in Fourth Wave Feminine Principles that honors the gifts of intuitive spiritual phenomena through these Holy Women's social action. This phenomenon turns the dominant paradigm on its head. Traditionally, male religious and philosophical writers, who are in the majority now but not for long, interpret religious literature by incorrectly measuring Holy Women's contribution by outer actions. This is partially a limitation only because the historic and cultural setting surrounding the woman's life was regarded and not the inner criteria for manifestation. This measurement qualified by a lack of written script, for example, fixes a Holy Woman into preset standards designed by male predecessors who were dominant in religious authority where writing and reading were limited to only a very few women historically. One has to ask the question as to whether male authority in the Judeo-Christian-Islamic and Buddhist religious development actually understands the inner gnosis of the Holy Mother of the World-Gaia since female oppression was prescribed in most religious doctrines worldwide. The Holy Women in this section, Hazrat Babajan, Julian of Norwich, Mary Baker Eddy, Sanapia, and Dr. Rina Sircar, were regarded as mystics, visionaries, prophets, healers, and masters of their generation. If there were doctrinal limitations that were operating behind their spiritual belief systems, it would be that these Holy Women forged against those externalized odds and challenged the inner exegesis of meaning found in altruistic action, compassion, love, and wisdom. These qualities will always be at the core mapping of the theophany (the Creative essence of the Divine Nature) of the world soul who is the Mother of the World-Gaia assisting her Creation.

In respect to the prevailing religious doctrines that originated from male-based revelation and doctrinal practices, I bow and honor all the Prophets of the World in the male form for they were also born from the Holy Mother of the World-Gaia. But there are more beings to know, and these I present in Chapter II as five Holy Women who offer insight into the resurgence of Divine Grace that speaks directly to Fourth Wave Feminism as they inaugurate the celestial soul of the Holy Mother of the World through mental accomplishment and intuitive gnosis. As the reader takes in the discovery of each Holy Women's intuitive process, let us not forget the oppressive forces that are externally limiting them. It is very much like the Sufis in the ancient world around Anatolia in the 5th century who were hunted and killed by leading Caliphs who were less universalized than the magnanimous Sufis. Instead of taking up arms in defense, they went underground and through esoteric secret societies, nonviolently, they kept alive the spiritual transmission of their awakened predecessors.

How one seeks to interpret the inner experiences of a prophetic heart, and explain it according to the perceiver (the reader) is the purpose of this next section. In the second section of this book, each woman's connection to spirit and accomplishment, regardless of the outer sociological conditions that suppressed her ability to function authentically, is addressed sociologically and regarded as a Divine initiation. To find correlative insight about their authentic contribution, it was necessary to source as much information, via their personal letters as was revealed, for example, in Mary Baker Eddy's non-published letters, and also practice meditative methods in person as I did with Dr. Rina Sircar. I also conferred with Sister Jose Hobday, an Iroquois teacher at the University of Creation Spirituality who explained many aspects of Native Indian spirituality.

When we regard mystical, transcendent transformation of the personal, spiritual illumination, prophetic utterances and actions of social justice, we might consider how to determine what the experiences mean to that Holy Women and then to oneself. How these experiences provide an essential structure for accessing one's process to spiritual gnosis is an important exploration of one's own spiritual path. Transcendental phenomenology, as explained in Chapter 1, provides a foundation to focus on meaning that sustains inner inquiry. The approach provides a structure for reflection and ways of knowing oneself that educates a person toward a remembrance of valuable phenomena that is as rich and multilayered as you are.

The five Holy Women in this section had information that was prophetically contributory to their faith and to the community around them as they spoke from divine inspiration. They reveal their mystical soul's mission that communicates the movement and work of the Holy Mother of the World-Gaia and is not common knowledge. They advocate salvific methods whose image of the human soul is constituted of the endowed celestial vision of faith, love and kindness that supports and uplifts the Holy Mother's Creation in all levels of manifestation.

Insight and prophetic utterance in the face of critical pain was Julian's contribution while giving us instructions in her "showings" of Christ as "Mother." Hazrat Babajan, a Sufi Dervish, foretold future events and lifted her own female identity to spiritual heights by living the itinerate life in a male-dominated Islamic culture only to enlighten future Avatars such as Pir-O-Murshid Hazrat Inayat Khan and Meher Baba. Sanapia-Comanche Eagle Doctor introduces us to her "roughing days" which are so important to hear for all of us who have paid a huge price for what we thought were our mistakes. Dr. Rina Sircar, Meditation Master, lays down the lines for organization of mind and execution of aggregate parts to the whole as found in Buddhist methods, with the accuracy of Divine accomplishment. These Five Holy Women bring us codes for our spiritual journey. For example, they indicate how subject relates to an object, how spirit relates to flesh, how private insight relates to common experience of a single woman in the past to many women in the present and which then reaches to all of humanity. These brief ideas encapsulate the next five Holy Women's ever-living prophetic contribution to the world.

Approaches: Sociological and Sufi Esoteric Considerations

To examine the different experiences of these Holy Women, I am primarily regarding sociological facts during the women's timeframe and secondarily using Sufi esoteric principles that identify their inspired inner state for the purpose of culling insight from the interpretive form of analysis. The mystical condition of perpetual self-disclosure ontologically indicates how one gives birth to the mystical and prophetic nature which is lasting and always present and never fixed on only one individual messenger during a generation of peoples but rather multiple individuals, particularly women who have offered themselves as instruments of the Divine Mother or archetypal examples of Her Being. The intention of the individual women's internal process is one of clear spiritual directedness or "intentionality" as Husserl (1977) states:

"Intentionality is the fundamental characteristic of psychic phenomena which is the groundwork for a descriptive transcendental philosophy of consciousness" [lxiii] by regarding certain classifications of phenomena.

The three phenomena I will be focusing on are:

---

1) The mystical nature that discovers the inner and outer meaning of spiritual connection through some sudden physical experience, and

2) The transformative breakthrough that changes the sociologically programmed aspects of the culture surrounding the individual,

3) The arising of prophetic vision and the action that follows the revelation.

To explain these three phenomena further we have to consider the following:

1) The mystical nature and phenomena of the intuitive discovery of self-disclosure both inner and outer set free the women from her sociological and religious prototyping by dominant paradigms. These paradigms that project upon women a hierarchal bias often limited women's psychic, religious, and spiritual activities in the world through the enforcement of gender profiling. For centuries, beginning in pre-Medieval Western societies in France, England, and Germany, and Middle Eastern societies such as in Saudi Arabian peninsula, Persia, and Afghanistan, sociological and religious rules of wifely behavior suppressed extraordinary and spiritually inclined women from living freely and spiritually directed lives. One can find these restrictions articulated in Jewish, Christian, and Islamic commentarial writings by male authors. The Holy Women reported in this study indicate how they attempted to break out of the socialized models of submission placed by either religious and cultural law usually set by patriarchal constituencies that denigrated women's spiritual authority.

2) The experience of breakthrough can be defined as a plastic consciousness as understood when the body, mind, and heart connect with all circumstances in human behavior. From this unified connection, one can find in the lives of these Holy Women's prophetic utterances or revelation from images describing Divine proximity. The Divine proximity became a pathway of inner attunement to their spiritual purpose, sometimes motivated by the desire to forewarn their community of danger as found in the life stories of Hazrat Babajan [lxiv] and to heal the sick as found in Mary Baker Eddy's collection of letters and Sanapia's instructions to keep the Medicine sacred. [lxv] The arising of prophetic vision or the action of revelation is an experience that is described by an absorption into an invisible world. An individual in the swoon of such an ecstatic

union has in their grasp only that which is meant for them such as one receives images in a dream, or paranormal messages that come from nature and bodily sensations. These messages are considered out of the range of the mundane mind.

3) The arising of prophetic vision have been written about in many religious commentaries and all seem to have a common thread and that is how the presence of the Divine brings great happiness and fulfillment to the soul of the individual. The prophetic beings that experience this proximity do not claim a greater happiness than others, knowing that all beings have shortcomings and limitations but this happiness directs the actions on the stage of life that remains in the constant presence of the Divine Source.

Religious Profiling of the Feminine

As I write about gender profiling in the following religious systems, I reflect on the situations they faced, the extreme bias and limitation that attempted to stop them when endeavoring to follow the map of their most exalted soul-blueprint. In this section I do not address the doctrinal limitations as feminist warfare but rather as a point of consideration to indicate the profound courage it takes to move ahead against the stream of the dominant paradigm. On the part of each Holy Woman in this text, I appeal to all believing people who hold the sacred view that each and every being is a Divine Manifestation of the Holy Mother of the World and that all might gaze upon women now and forevermore as a free soul partner in this life.

Ancient Hebrew-Judaic Cultural Prototype of the Feminine

In the Ancient Hebrew-Judaic Culture women's roles were defined in the family and the home. Ceremonies that were usually led by women such as the sanctification of the Sabbath, fest of Tabernacles and the Seder meal at Passover, the lighting of the Hanukkah candles were all led in the home by women and not in the Synagogue. The rabbinic movement, around the first seven centuries CE, codified the customs and gender expectations especially found in worship, study, and public leadership that became prioritized toward the male.

Women were not allowed education or marital free choice, and she faced pressured expectation to bear many children after an arranged marriage. Throughout the centuries, women's hierarchal status in the home was downgraded by the rise of ecclesiastical institutionalism, similar to Christian models, and the home which was the women's singular step to equality was eroded and lost its significance while the prohibitions by rabbinic order became more restrictive and the male leadership grew stronger.

In some mystical communities such as in Spain, where one finds the Sephardic traditions, and in Western and Central European communities, where Ashkenazi Jewish groups formed, the women were elevated to the position of "spiritual consort" through the element of the Shekinah awareness of love that softened the pejorative Yahweh in Kabbalistic study but demonized as one who menstruates which excluded her from mystical participation and leadership.

Organization and conceptualized religious conduct predicated over the community on every level of human existence, and with this locus of religious law dominating in all aspects of life, a form of male democracy arose but not for the women. Still in the modern era that the Amanuensis Frida Waterhouse encountered in her story, these cultural aspects were operative.

It is true that human behavior found in the Hebrew-Judaic ancient culture was met with the positive experience of bringing the male Creator God into every activity of life. These laws were essentially salvific for the change in the communities' behavior as it brought greater respect and caring but at the same time the eulogies that proclaimed holiness were often broken apart by the obsession with proscribed minute details such as how to dress, wash, eat, pray, and sleep, forgetting the human population came into life through the presence of the Holy Mother of the World which would have changed the attitude of Divine disclosure that could actualize the democratization for both genders and affirm the unification of the Holy Mother's creation.

Medieval Christian Gender Profiling

In Medieval Christian societies, particularly that which surrounded Julian of Norwich, female gender restrictions predominated over Medieval Christian practices. Conservative Christian practices ostracized women because of their body functions, such as when women were prevented from attending Catholic Mass when she menstruated. Augustine, the proponent of original sin, wrote codes that relegated women to low regard and developed a critical hatred for women's physical bodies because they caused men to have erections and made them lose control. [lxvi]

One can question why men of all levels of intelligence never challenged the male hierarchy of the church that advocated rules against women without applying the same rules of self-control over men's libidinal forces? Rather than institute regulations of control on men, all women were considered to be the negative impulses that stimulated men sexually, and a deprivation of spiritual balance became the formulation of hundreds of years of misguided religious history the world has ever known, called the Dark Ages of Christendom. The marginalization of women was an easy "*domination strategy*" by church fathers who followed in the distorted principles of Augustine that were formed in the Malleus Maleficarum document during the witch-hunting Inquisition in the same period. Although arguments can be found about Augustine's love of his mother and his history of maintaining mistresses during his lifetime, he felt that sex was a primary locus of sin. He reveals a Neo-Platonic neurosis about all things that concern the body. Plato's devaluation of the feminine was explicit and was followed up in Aristotle's theorization that the women contributed the more primitive and material principle to the embryo but denied that the man's contribution also was of a material sort. Instead, Aristotle held that the masculine contribution was more spiritual and divine. [lxvii] From a post-modern perspective, this is utterly laughable.

Augustine's attitude on sex seems to indicate an attempted desire to transcend the physical form and to be free of the physical bodies corruptibility. It is no surprise that Augustine was considered the spiritual father of the Puritans in America and from which Calvinism departs a bit in favor of women's position.

The departure from Augustine's attitudes was how Calvinism (John Calvin 1519-1564), which antedates the Reformation, aimed to reform church and society on the model of both classical and Christian antiquity by bringing in a Protestant revolution and returning to humanistic understanding of the Christian Scripture. Calvin's humanism influenced his thought in several basic ways. His primary insight is that he shared with earlier Renaissance humanists an essentially biblical conception of the human personality, comprehending it not as a hierarchy of faculties ruled by reason but as a mysterious unity in which what is primary is not what is highest but what is central, and that was the heart. This conception assigned more importance and a sense of dignity to the body. For this reason, Calvin rejected the ascetic disregard of the body's basic needs that was often negated in medieval spirituality. Implicit in this particular rejection included the traditional hierarchy of faculties in the personality; however, it was a radical rejection of the traditional belief that hierarchy was the basis of order. For Calvin, the only foundation for order in human affairs was utility. Among its other consequences, this position undermined the traditional one subordinating women to men. Calvin believed that, for practical reasons, it may be necessary for some to command and others to obey, but it could no longer be argued that women must naturally be subordinated to men. Calvin believed that every occupation in society is a "calling" on the part of God who sanctified these conceptions. Overall, Calvin recognized that God is commonly experienced as a mother. He denounced those who represent God as dreadful; God for him was *"mild, kind, gentle, and compassionate."* He felt that human beings could never praise God enough until God *"wins us by sweetness and goodness."*[lxviii]

Although Calvinism was leading a distinctive shift away from medieval practices that threatened women's lives, the contributions of women's mystical experiences, educational excellence, herbal knowledge, healing practices through midwifery, and prophetic insight endangered their existence. When they revealed their compassionate skills they were exterminated as evidenced by the eight million women who were victimized and killed during the Inquisition under the rampant lies fostered as "*black magic*" by the Catholic Church. The Church's advocacy of female suppression by intimidation, threatened their social place in the community. The eradication of women's written contribution to spiritual understanding and humanistic practices that support healing must have been copious because there were many literate women in Medieval Christian European countries, as one can find the work of the Christian Beguines: Hildegard von Bingen, Mechthild de Magdeburg, Marguerite Porete, and Hadewijch of Antwerp, to name a few. The pervasive bias against women's menstrual or menopausal phases, the insistence on virginity as an idealized state, and the social penalties on women who do not marry and bear children with no official avenues for work except indentured servitude, or prostitution, all composed the societal codification of wifely status that kept women from becoming free women. The composition of a systemized strategy forms the intense scenario surrounding women's choices for offering her mystical and prophetic vision and yet...even against these conditions, the mystical visions arose, the prophetic nature evolved, the healing work continued, and the Holy Divine Mother emerged through the suppression.

Suspicion for women's equality and mystical contribution held firmly in Christianity up into the 17th century. It is rare but we can find in French Christian historical literature in the same century communities where one could observe a deeper schism about the standards of enforced religious behavior placed upon the female worshipper of a Christian faith system, from pure obedience to doctrinal regulation of their bodies' function to that of unexpected mystical awakening which was sometimes supported by an unusual male practitioner. It was with the Quietist movement led by François Fenelon, archbishop of Cambrai, who was condemned by the Church because he emphasized pure mystical love over that of ecclesiastical practice. [lxix]

In the ecstatic utterances of the mystic love, an extraordinary power exists, and the Church found these utterances threatening. Fenelon offers the exception to the general inclination of strict obedience to church doctrine. He was supporting what women were trying to break away from in Church doctrine, mandating close obedience to regulations that proclaimed the body as sinful. The regulations were formed to control the populace through purgative actions, and he too died when he turned against such claims.

Because arranged marriages were common practice and enforced by the father of a family with a female child usually under the age of 14 to an older man, only by deliberate resistance on the part of the women, sometimes risking her well-being, could they rebel against the socialized expectation of a woman's obedience to her father or family. As an alternative in Christianity, the young girl could offer her dowry to the Church and join a convent or monastic order that would protect her from unwanted marriage and pregnancies. But as we know through historic documents from nuns and cloistered women, the protection did not exist.

Of course, even anchorites, such as Julian of Norwich, had to pass the scrutiny of a male bishop to enter the convent. However, with a generous donation the Church became the custodian of the woman's entire endowment. The woman's life had to be chaste and simple, and she was to give up all ease and comforts even though paying a great financial price. Under the most severe conditions, in her small and unheated cell in Conesford Street, Julian contributed some of the rarest and insightful mystical revelations from the 14th century. (See following section: Julian of Norwich)

Medieval Muslim Gender Profiling

In early Medieval Muslim communities during the time before the arising of Prophet Mohammed (SAAwS) (570-632 AD.), female infanticide was practiced with dominant paradigm cultural attitudes favoring male children. Education was not favored for female children and religious practice was relegated behind closed quarters especially designed for women, who were kept in segregated areas. This attitude still exists in 21st century contemporary culture, particularly in tribal areas of Saudi Arabia and as practiced by the Wahhabi sect and the Taliban in Afghanistan. Women could not inherit land or property from her parents and usually were pressured into arranged marriages and treated like property by the men, particularly the father, who tried to marry their daughters off to the wealthiest suitor. The Taliban imitate Wahhabism by instituting constrictive practices that threaten women's liberty and prevent education. Veiling, repression, restriction of free expression, and domestic violence persist as a dominating principle that submerges feminine equality and have institutionalized aberrant principles that hold back the evolution of spiritual actualization in women.

99

Regardless of the arguments that support these types of feminine restriction, such as the argument of feminine modesty, they all fall short of one major evolutionary awareness, and that is, that every composite being formed of X and Y chromosomes is in essence a manifest body of One Divine Being, and in fact the Fatima-Sophia is the Soul of Creation and the constitutive part of the Holy Qur'an.

Under these despotic regimes, if women did not abide by veiled dress codes and orthodox constraint, their lives would be in jeopardy. Women have been forced to rationalize restriction by even considering them as a point of respect for the society that inflicts upon them such restrictive regulations. A woman curtails her choices so that she would not seem disrespectful to the general population of women who gave up their free choices years ago and found a way to live with them. In the majority of Muslim societies, women are still not able to pray in the same room as men. This remains a stigmatizing choice set into law by the Ulema (religious authority) who authorized Fatwas to control the female population's behavior in the culture and in the Mosque. However, after the arising of the Prophet who said, *"Women are the twin halves of men"* using the metaphor of the protective garment of clothing as way of providing protection for each other, [lxx] because of the Holy Prophet's love and fairness, the cultural stigma of limitation changed for the better in some communities. It must be stated at this point that commentaries on the Qur'anic meaning require utter discernment as to the deeper contemplation and meaning of the Holy Prophet's words. Tribal practices that manipulated Qur'anic meaning still pervade many communities in the Middle Eastern and Western regions and exclusionary gender-biased practices exist in modern Muslim society to this day and yet much is changing.

Although Qur'anic Iyas (verses) offer direction for change to respect women's choices, such as the following:

"O you who have attained to faith (meaning you who have become Muslims) it is not lawful for you to try to become heirs to your wives' inheritance against their will; and neither shall you keep them under constraint with the view of taking away anything of what you may have given them, unless it be that they have become guilty, in an obvious manner, of immoral conduct. And consort with your wives in a goodly manner; for if you dislike them, it may well be that you dislike something which God might yet make a source of abundant good."[lxxi]

This Iya (verse) only applies to women as wives; there is much to be considered in how the Prophet Mohammed (SAAwS) respected free women as he did Khadija, when he met her and later they married. Khadija, who was an independent and wealthy businesswoman, added much to his understanding of equality in a time when women were disempowered because of their gender. Let us not forget, Khadija hired Mohammed to run her business trips that transported merchandise around the Saudi Arabian peninsula. She respected his honesty and was the first to recognize his prophetic aural transmissions from the Angel Gabriel. It is very possible that, without her accurate intuitive insight, he would not have realized the efficacy of his own prophetic visionary experience. Within Khadija's inner prophetic development, she opened the way for him to understand the external inspiration (*Wahy Zahir*) which the Mystics such as Sheikh Jiwan Ahmad (AH 1130) have spoken about concerning the angelic messages the Holy Prophet was to bring to the people at a time when tribal conflict was at its most destructive impasse.

There are three mystical approaches of understanding the external inspiration (*Wahy Zahir*). The mouth of an angel gives the first mystical approach. In Prophet Mohammed's case it was the Angel Gabriel whom he heard and established the faith in him that knew it as Divine proximity. The second approach was the awareness that the Holy Spirit breathed into his heart (*Wahy Batin*), and the third is the light of prophecy that which is a kind of inspiration saints and mystics talk about as the inner transformation of mystical unity *(Tawhid).* lxxii

It is suggested in many spiritual writings it was Khadija's prophetic development which recognized the sign that Mohammed was inspired, she understood how completely absent he was, though remaining in physical form. She noticed his respiration was strenuous and he seemed to have been in a cataleptic fit or swoon. In reality, she perceived this as an absorption into the invisible world she understood deeply.

Although women such as Khadija had attained spiritual development, the difficulty female mystics faced was due to the religious succession of men and therefore women had to become wives, hermits, or solitary dervishes, such as the difficult circumstances found in Hazrat Babajan's life in Afghanistan. Hazrat Babajan lived without the comforts provided by the systems of preceptors (*pirs*) in the lineages who could judge one's conduct lxxiii designed by men for men. Under the religious interpretation of Hadith, used for the purpose of bringing fixity to laws that were backed by fatwas distributed by the Caliph (spiritual head) or Ulema (leading religious teachers), women were kept under tight restriction and which disallowed their spiritual authority. If a fatwa was signed by a leading religious male figure against the women in question this could lead to her death or incarceration. As only Muslim men are placed in stations of religious authority and women are not allowed to participate in council, this arrangement cancels out any level ground for balance in spiritual or even secular evaluation.

Descent of Spiritual authorship from the Caliphate involves an investiture charter, of which Fatima Mernissi says, *"History teaches us that the Caliph is always a man, and women are unworthy of exercising even an inferior kind of power, such as mulk, basely secular power."* lxxiv

The Caliph was historically considered the representative of God on earth and welded Divine authority in all matters. Usually all women were denied spiritual authority, and even in secular matters the Caliph usually denied his blessings upon any woman. Mernissi firmly states that the entire Muslim hierarchy, in all matters of spiritual and secular authority, must be a linked with the Divine, however pro forma it may be. lxxv

A constant reiteration of restriction and mechanical perfunctory practice in Muslim history from the upholders of orthodoxy saw every occasion that a woman claimed power as an aggressive violation of the rules of the game. The authority of the orthodoxy changed at different times depending on the power of the sword and extortion of taxes. However, as soon as a woman appeared on the scene and challenged the authority in the name of spiritual authority or Shari'a, she was taken out. Mernissi continues to say that the ability of women to manage something "lesser" (meaning secular) is disputed, it goes without saying that their candidature to manage something "greater" (meaning spiritual) would not be considered because any innovation about the derailment of the narrow path of Shari'a comes back to Ibn Rushd's (known in Latin as Averroes) comment that *"Women have no power and are under the control of men."* [lxxvi] All Muslims respect and consider the work of Ibn Rushd-Averroes because he was one of the truly famous religious philosophers of the Islamic tradition and Greek thought whose copious manuscripts detail the argument between religious laws and philosophy. His commentaries on Aristotle's work are legendary and have been studied by scholars all over the world. Ibn Rushd's bold claim says that only the metaphysician employing certain proof (syllogism) is capable and competent as well as obliged to interpret the doctrines contained in the prophetically revealed law or Shari'a and not Muslim theologians who rely on dialectical arguments. He firmly believed that philosophy was the only pathway into the inner meaning of religious belief in the quest for truth. The inner meaning must not be divulged to the masses or to women, but only those external meanings of Scriptures contained in stories, meanings, and metaphors should be accepted by the masses without argument. Although Ibn Rushd brought great synthesis to the Arab and Greek world, he brought great strife to the cause of women and to the Holy Mother-Gaia's love of Her creation.

Western Models of 18th Century Female Profiling

Late 18th century and early 19th century profiling of women, which activated into First Wave Feminism, was a time which was focused on officially mandated inequities that hampered women's political voice and found outer direction by getting women the vote (suffragettes). Standards of limitation absenting women from all levels of political, cultural, and religious leadership set the stage for repressive action toward those women who broke open that standard. Mary Daly (1928-2010) emphasized that the moral issue that needed to be addressed was the release of women from inequities that regarded her as fundamentally inferior but also laying claim to moral and spiritual authority over the community of believers. She says, *"The symbol of the Father God, spawned in the human imagination and sustained as plausible by patriarchy, has in turn rendered services to the type of society by making its mechanisms for the oppression of women appear right and fitting. If God in 'his' heaven is a father ruling 'his' people, then it is in the 'nature' of things and according to divine plans and of the order of the universe that society is male-dominated."*[lxxvii] The patriarchal consensus inhibiting feminine equality appears present in almost every religious doctrine. It is profoundly destructive and requires confrontation and devoted work toward the integration of both gender qualities within the body, heart and mind. The principles for Fourth Wave Feminism today, more than ever before, needs to arise for the needed awakening of humanity and the balancing within each and every individual so that the true pathway into the Holy Mother of the World-Gaia's arms is assured.

Value Changes in 18th and 19th Century Western Culture

Sociology is a study of human behavior that investigates the nature, causes, and effects of social relations among individuals. Although the analysis of society had been a part of Western culture since the ancient Greeks, the modern science of human feelings and emotions did not develop until the 18th and 19th centuries. Linking to other social sciences, it was considered a part of moral philosophy and was strongly influenced by Darwin's theory of biology and evolution. But it was Emile Durkheim who set the differentiations between psychology and biology by proposing that there were distinctive qualities or what he called "social facts," such as feelings, beliefs, rituals, and institutions of belief, that result from social intercourse and are not only found in individuals but rather that these external facts exert control over individual actions and behavior.

How perception of the world develops in the individual, through sight, hearing, sensorial conditions, logic, understanding of how change is regarded, and mechanically complex transactions and intuitional awareness, compose further elements of complex patterns of group interaction. Grouping together the cognitive systems of awareness stimulates and challenges individuals in their formative years when intuitional capacity is more active and unfettered by external concerns. Evidence of the effects of early intuitional inspiration reveals itself when a prophetic individual undertakes a leadership role in their community where concepts are rigidly aligned against them. This can be found in the life of Mary Baker Eddy who is the founding Prophet of the Christian Science Church. Women were never considered as prophets in the early 19th century.

Our sociological programming is selective in its values particularly when an individual sees themselves through the male hierarchal values that are inherently conditioned into the behavior of a group. Some conservative ideologies legitimated the status quo and thereby prevented social reform. Their belief, along with the notion that the stratification system selected the most aggressive and brilliant individuals to meet society's needs, supports the male-dominant paradigm. This was certainly the criticism by those alerted to sociological consideration that structural fundamentalism had to be addressed and reviewed critically in America and in other places in the world once First

Wave, Second Wave, and Third Wave Feminism got off the ground. Relationships in the group are networking elements; if they are confined in the dominant paradigm, a prophetic individual might find great difficulty living an authentic life. A woman cannot change one factor without affecting a great many other factors causing conflict, as Lewis A. Coser proclaimed that conflict ultimately fosters social cohesiveness either supporting or against the individual. [lxxviii] For example, the biological basis for socialization aims at understanding parent-youth relationships, peer group stimulation, and the basic personality, sex, and temperament that arises in individual development and has triggers on how that individual will relate to the group. Margaret Mead calls this factor "the acting self," and *"the I."* She then termed that part of the self that participates in the larger organization of the internalized attitudes of others *"the me."* [lxxix]

Enlargement of the self is dependent upon and in turn supports the breadth of community values. This outcome can be seen very clearly in the life of Sanapia, Comanche Eagle Doctor, who struggled toward a higher calling. Just as a child learns certain attitudes toward herself and others, that prescribed attitude is distinctively social in nature. As a child matures and is able to place herself in the role of the other, she responds to the world as she anticipates the world would respond to her. As the male-dominated approach of traditional stratification pressures [lxxx] a woman to act according to her subsumed purpose, a miraculous occurrence arises. I theorize that the ignorance of group attitudes upon a burgeoning Holy Soul sometimes actuates the emergence of the Holy Mother of the World-Gaia into presence, and a prophet is born.

As an individual learns and matures, a being can develop a unity of self thus seeing the world more as a reflection of a collective nature; one's gender and one's state of awakening no longer become the essential factor. The prophetic archetype embraces the view of the greater cosmic or non-dual awareness and knows the consequences of dualistic attitudes that set *"the acting self, the I"* against *"the me."* The non-dual realization gives them the distinctive wisdom to fasten their actions to a moral ideal that is expanded in consciousness and becomes a natural adhesive for the community to work together. Living the ethical Buddhist ideal, we can find in the life and work of Dr. Rina Sircar offering a non-dual awareness through the Abhidhamma methods that detail the deconstruction of material reality. The Buddhist Abhidhamma opens the consciousness to greater social mindfulness such as found in charity (*Dana*) and the virtues (*Sila*) and the healing potential that arises through meditation (*Vipassana*). Other deconstructive methods guide us on how to refuse being captured by outer dominant paradigm forms of social structuring.

Sociological standards that are predominantly controlled by the male gender fail in its approach to adhere community in a non-dual theology. This is evident in how women have been treated over the generations of male leadership in many of the cultures and religions in the world's history. Religious and/or cultural values that are inherently conditioned into the group by the dominant male hierarchy make use of religious laws to benefit self-promotion of male values. If we regard our social relationships as organizational lines in which mystically inclined individuals find themselves in an existing closed system that disagree with the social stratification, these women will inevitably experience some degree of repression from the dominant systems that divide by gender, race, religion, and philosophic variables.

A New Principle

The Holy Women in this Second Section provide a new vision. They perceived a ray of inspiration from the same source that male prophets received it, but they had to deal with a social stratification whose religious protocol was unequal because of gender restrictions as stated above. Sufi Mystics (Hazrat Inayat Khan, Rumi, Hafiz, and Kabir) say that self-disclosure as intimacy with the Divine source is within the mystical state of Divine unity (*Tawhid*) and it is a gift to the soul and given to every human being. This state does not dualistically separate the garden from the rose, or as Julian of Norwich called *"oneing,"* [lxxxi] the vision that brings Divine proximity. This proximity becomes the *"summum bonum,"* or source of Spiritual liberation within any spiritual or religious person, and it is never delegated to a gender but only to a soul that is ready to receive it. If we regard the definition of religion as stemming from *"religio,"* we would find it has its root in *"religare,"* which means, *"to bind again."* This terminology has reference to one's connection either to *"the acting self as I"* and *"the me"* which Margaret Mead coined with a spirit that honors a greater cosmic understanding than what our confined consciousness allows us to know in the moment under the dominant paradigm that we are presently living in.

There exists little consensus among scholars about what constitutes spiritual belief or religious faith but most certainly personal and social behavior identifies what religion is: *"Religion is concerned with behaviors, but it also has concepts about what inspires the behaviors or 'drives' them. Generally speaking, what drives religious systems and their various organizational activities and beliefs are some conceptualizations of a power or extraordinary reality, whether this is perceived as transcendent or immanent moving within the world."* [lxxxii]

It is the naming power that each religion maintains and codifies from the male prophet's utterance that calls a heart and mind to a spiritual attunement and thus to spiritual transcendence, which gives evidence to the esoteric development in an individual but is fabricated to support the dominant structure that perpetuates it.

What Margaret Mead brings into consideration is how different sociocultural perceptions, particularly of women, and their experiences are key factors in how religious groups see women in their context and give a functioning role to them. Franzmann is in agreement as she indicates: *"Religious systems cannot operate in a vacuum outside of the cultural expression and language as the religious function of any member is bound totally to the whole life of the community. There is always a vast variety within any tradition, influenced by two-way process of the religion adapting to the cultural setting and receiving cultural and folk accretions in return. In relation to women, then, this means that where women are limited by aspects of a particular culture or folk system, those aspects may also have their effect eventually within religious tradition, or perhaps the religious tradition will include such aspects from the very beginning."* [lxxxiii]

Julian of Norwich, Hazrat Babajan, Mary Baker Eddy, Sanapia, and Dr. Sircar hold a wider consciousness than the two points stated by Franzmann concerning religious adaptation to cultural setting and receiving cultural folk accretions in return.

110

They expanded out from the concepts that formed their closed religious structure. They followed their inner voice; they chose freedom for their soul to act in the world while benefiting all those around them. These Holy Women show us how wisdom nature is a natural adhesive when regarding diverse cultural paths and confining gender belief systems. As we begin to become familiar with their lives, their decisions, their visions, and their suffering within their cultural setting, we realize how deeply they were fastened to their true spiritual work and the inner vision that motivated them which they were destined to bring into the world. Their words and experiences could be seen as a transcendence of their cultural concepts and even their religious doctrine, which they honored.

There arises an agreement among these Holy Women, that the existence of an extraordinary power lives within our souls, but how it is mediated or accessed under the conditions of their sociological and religious repression, which was wholly defined by the dominating powers within their existing doctrines, becomes an important point of analysis in the stories of these next five Holy Women. Yet how they created the image of their inspirer, how they manifested that image in their life, becomes a testimony of true reverence for the Holy Mother of the World-Gaia and the manner in which she works. In order to explain this further, I turn to esoteric Sufi principles that guide us into the inner state of the soul.

Sufi Esoteric Principles for Examining the Inner State, the Soul

In Sufi mystical writings, which historically have always attempted to find unity in religious purpose rather than conform to accepted rituals reflecting societies cultural standards, one can find in the exegetical writings of the 20th century Sufi mystic Hazrat Inayat Khan a valuable explanation for esoteric understanding of the soul. He says, "*The path of this journey is within ourselves; just like the wide space beheld by the eyes, which do not seem more than an inch wide, yet miles of horizon can be reflected in them. It is so wide, and there is a path that runs from the body to the soul, from the human being to God.*" [lxxxiv]

Women and men who deepen their inherent mystical nature within their consciousness and who participate in their chosen religious group eventually will be drawn to this expanded perspective. Mystics practice self-surrender of the ego nature (*Fana*) not by using physical limitation such as celibacy imposed by religious doctrinal regulations. They do not seek to know themselves through the "*ummah*" (Muslim spiritual community), the Christian congregation, or the Buddhist Sangha. Neither do their intuitive experiences, impressed into their heart, as Sufis call the (*Wahy Zahir*), conditionally change the limited sociological circumstance in which the mystic might find himself or herself during their historic timeframe. Rather the Sufi, whose mystical insight is intuitively illuminated, becomes awakened by a physical condition such as found in a state of internal inspiration (*Wahy Batin*). This empathic state embraces those that may very well be the cause of their limitation. A non-dual connection such as this brings the individual's cognitive, somatic, and emotional experiences into connection with all human experiences. In this way the universalized experiences are made whole and brought into Unity (*Tawhid*), and this spiritual state informs those who are ready to understand, the connection the Great Mother of the World-Gaia has with her Creation. These Holy Women, brought forward in Chapter II then offer the prophetic legacies of the soul, their mystical wisdom as notes adding to a great symphony.

Non-dual spiritual experience can be found as a seed in many of the major Avatar's experience. In Sufism it is termed, *"Fana-fi-Illah,"* or effacement in the One Divine Being; in Christianity it is the heart of love (*Agapé*); in Hindu Upanishads, it is found at "I am that I am" (*"Sat vam asi"*). The non-dual experience, the mystical *"I am"* is synonymous with the Creator. Non-dual consciousness is not a particular experience of gender per se but rather a conscious state that declares the very essence and purpose of life by activating one's life energy toward intensified service to the World's Creation that came through the Holy Mother-Gaia. What the ancient male prophets left in the world was a sense of their insight and conscious awakening. The existing rituals and rules that came later after the Avatar departed gave a particular religion its quality, but it seems that the historic majority did not grasp the inner refinements of the Avatar's gnosis. When the deeper inner realization of how the Mother of the World-Gaia works in the human soul, albeit female or male, we begin to awaken to the theophany and proximity of Her Holy Divine nature and to the resurrection of the earth. That awareness is only found in the purest sense of absorption. This transformed state can lift the soul to another station of awakened consciousness and in turn allow one to be in the world in the most unified sense, but not captured by the individuality of the world's characters which cannot perceive how all Creation is a precious inseparable unfolding of Her Holy Being.

Chapter II

Mystical Illumination, Accomplishment, Prophetic Utterances, and Social Justice

Julian of Norwich (Medieval Christian Mystic)

Mary Baker Eddy (Christian Science Prophet and Founder)

Hazrat Babajan (Parthan Sufi Mystic)

Sanapia (Comanche Eagle Doctor)

Dr. Rina Sircar (Buddhist Meditation Master)

Thirty spokes meet in the hub, but it is upon the empty space, the non-existent, in the hub that the wheel's usefulness depends. Kneading clay, one molds vessels of it, but only their hollowness, the non-existent, makes their filling possible. With walls from which doors and windows are cut out, a house is built. But only its empty space, the non-existent, gives it its value; the visible, the existent, gives form to the work. The invisible, the non-existent, give it essence and meaning. lxxxv

Introductory Remarks

To gain insight into the overarching mystical experiences of these five Holy Women, I have hermeneutically sourced their viewpoint about their lives through their biographical literature, letters, interviews, commentarial texts if it exists, and by autobiographical writings and interviews by those who met them or practiced their methods as well as considering the correlative spiritual literature of their religious belief system. Hazrat Babajan, for example, does not have any autobiographical material, as she did not write, but historical information does exist. Julian of Norwich has written a great deal about her "Showings" and I have revealed how she perceived Christ Jesus as the nurturing mother. I have also compared Julian's mystical revelations with the Rule of St. Benedict, which presented standardizations for preserving contemplative community life. Mary Baker Eddy's copious written works were graciously available to me at the Christian Science Library in Boston, Massachusetts. The material in this book is extracted from her private letters, manuscripts, and publications. Dr. Rina Sircar reveals her accomplishment and understanding in the compilation of commentaries on the Abhidhamma Sutta, revealing years of masterful meditation practice with her teacher, Taungpulu Tawya Kabe Aye Sayadaw from Burma (Rangoon). For Sanapia, there is only one interview source because she did not write but rather relied on the oral transmission given to the author of a book in her name, which is most compelling and is notated in the bibliography. I have referenced the biographical documents of the Sufi Matriarch, Hazrat Babajan of Afghanistan, and compared her mystical experiences with the Sufi mystical writings of Hazrat Inayat Khan, a master teacher who came to the West in 1910 delivering a new message of Spiritual Liberty that arose from the ancient major Sufi lineages (tariqahs), the Chisti, Naqshabandi, Suhrwardi, and Qadiri Orders.

Foundational Sufi Literature

I have also referenced Sheikh Jiwan Ahmad's (1130 A.H.) *The Light of Inspiration (Nuru-l'Anwar)* and the mystical text by Abu Hamid-al-Ghazzali (1111 A.H.), *The Niche of Lights (Mishkat al-Anwar)*, will be referenced for the valuable descriptions of the supreme Adept who ascends to Divine Unity through the awareness of how to see light through the eyes which is external to that of the light that shines upon pure intelligence into the World of the internal Celestial Realm. The Sufis guide us to the moment when the light dawns and one begins to actually see after having before only sensed potentially. [lxxxvi] The Sufi mystical writings do not reflect gender separation. They are written to propose a single purpose, which is that of the illuminated heart.

This single purpose is also reflected in the writings of Hazrat Inayat Khan (1964)—the Sufi Message Volumes, *Philosophy, Psychology, and Mysticism*. This text forms the foundational ground for understanding mystical experiences because they indicate no prejudice concerning how human beings experience the ineffable. How a person seeks self-knowledge within and without is a point of contemplative importance toward revealing how a mystic functions within the wider consciousness in both female and male incarnation. For Hazrat Inayat Khan, it is not self-knowledge that only arises from the organs of intuition but unitive awareness. Therefore, the human body is a perfect instrument as it is prepared to receive all levels of sensory and ultra-sensory impressions such as found in the nervous system and the heart.

Sufi masters from all lineages generally regard human beings as manifestations of divine wisdom, the highest attribute of God appearing under different names and forms; and they love them with all adoration, as the lover loves the Beloved in all different garments, and throughout all stages of life. Inayat Khan says, *"What a great treasure it is when a [human being] has realized that in [their being] are to be found all the merits and all the faults which exist in the world, and that they can cultivate all they wish to cultivate, and cut away all that should be removed! It is like rooting out all the weeds and sowing the seed of flowers and fruits. One finds that all is in oneself, and that one can cultivate in oneself all that one wishes. A world opens for the [person] who begins to look within themselves; for it is not a little plot of ground that he or she has to cultivate; [they] have a world to make of [themselves], and to make a world is sufficient occupation to live for."* (Parenthesis mine) [lxxxvii]

Though the mystic's desire for self-actualization [lxxxviii] is related to self-realization, there is an attraction to the unknown and toward independence. When a state of self-actualization and realization arises, the heart increases its capacity and becomes microcosmic and macrocosmic at the same time, thus increasing freedom.

The vision of the world is like a drop in the ocean of the infinite, and yet within that drop all things exist. All those who have brought wisdom to the world were self-actualized, self-realized beings. The sages and saints, mystics and prophets experienced old stimuli with fresh and newly born appreciation for insight. They effaced themselves by fully recognizing the potential of spirit in materiality as consciousness, which is their

118

divine purpose living within their connections, feelings, perceptions, volitions, and desires. That Divine purpose is the unity principle (*Tawhid*), which to the Sufis means the complete connectivity of everything to everything else which is from the Divine Source. This awareness is an opportunity within perception that all beings have within them when given birth into human form.

The human form in a woman's body offers a spiritual transmission that is theophonically connected and always unified to the Creator. It is impossible to conceive of any being extrinsic to absolute being. She produces within her own body the Divine mediation between the states of knowledge that have descended upon the human form from the Celestial and then to the global society. There is a great need for deeper understanding of what is really going on within the incarnation process and that, which is not yet understood about human embodiment, because it comes from realms not yet known. Through Julian, Mary Baker Eddy, Hazrat Babajan, Sanapia, and Rina Sircar's experiences in the human form, a universal language is embedded in their challenges not only through the societies' negation of their essential being but how they met these limitations is truly inspiring. With the gifts of their intelligence, wisdom, and intuitive skill, they gave us the path of ontological superiority. These five Holy Women direct us to the Celestial Being. These stories that follow are the manifestations of the Holy Mother of the World who went beyond the World to help the world as they offer love and a different realm of existence.

Julian of Norwich (1342 – ca. 1416) - The Hidden Visionary

Julian was an anchorite (recluse) in a Benedictine convent of Carrow. The church on this site dates back to as early as 950, making it the oldest foundation in the City. It has gone through many changes and attacks on its structure by Danish invaders in 1004, to becoming merchant's houses in the late 18th century, to being bombed in World War II. Yet fragments remain in the church's history, and in Julian's will she offers a view of the cell she lived in for 40 years. Now it is a place where many can visit and take pilgrimage.

There is little about her personal life, but it is known that she is one of the first medieval women who wrote a book in the English language, although due to the sociological circumstances of women during her history, she was not published and she lived as an anchoress in one room or monastic cell. She was uneducated and might have been married, widowed, and had children. When she was 30 years old, in 1373, during a severe illness that almost took her to the door of death, she received a series of 16 'showings' (visions) about the passion of Christ on which she spent the next 20 years writing them down and meditating upon them. She called these 'showings' "The Revelation of Divine Love." These writings are considered the greatest spiritual medieval classics in existence and reveal no wrathful perception in the Divine Godhead but rather look upon the nature of the Godhead as a loving, compassionate mother.

Julian is an unlikely prophet of her time because she was one of the first who regarded Christ in the Feminine archetype. She perceived sin as some kind of sickness and offered one of the first intuitional approaches to salvation as a process of self-actualization. The point being that she recognizes sin as not a fault in human character, per se, but rather a sickness that needed healing. Thus the tender, feminine side of God is clear in her mantra, "All shall be well and all manner of things shall be well again." Her mantra became a powerful clarion call for those who faced all kinds of challenges due to social instability in the political climate of the medieval period. A male vindictive God (Yahweh) plagued human beings with eternal punishment in the fires of hell. Julian lifted up humanity by her true feminine vision of Godhead as "Mother."

Julian's entire legacy counters the Augustinian premise that we were all born in sin and must spend the rest of our lives redeeming ourselves. Here, Julian's insight leads us to experience the mystical heart embracing all beings as Divine creation from the same loving Mother (the Christ), which echoes the work of post-modern Liberation

Theologians such as Matthew Fox, Leonardo Boff, Mary Daly, and Marie Pilar Aquino whose call *"to live praxis as faith's verification"*; [lxxxix] and here with Julian's visions we can regard *"hermeneutical viewpoint as the structural horizon for theological knowledge"* as she brings us to a deeper sense through allegories which was a remarkable characteristic of ancient exegesis.

Julian's theology changes the course of patriarchy in Christianity. She brings us hope in understanding the meaning of pain and how it will be relieved. Her portrait of Christ is filled with images of blood and sacrifice, but she sees this as the connective awareness with all elements in each one of our lives in which a sense of recovery can emerge through the process of redemptive transformation, meaning to free oneself from distress. It is a disturbing message but one that has in it common transformative results for all actions that are harmful to others and ourselves. She says, *"We must needs fall, and we must needs see it. If we did not fall, we would never find out on our own how weak and wretched we are, nor would we know so fully our Maker's marvelous love."* [xc]

Many things have to suffer crucifixion, as Jesus did, as he remains the central figure in Julian's showings. The great contribution Jesus offers Julian is his obedience to fulfill the mission he understood necessary in human form as all things work together for God. She says, *"Suddenly you will be taken from your pain, from all your sickness, from all this disease, and from all this woe. And you shall come up above, and you shall have me as your reward, and you will be filled full of love and bliss."* [xci]

Through pain, she brings her great insight to bear against the passage of a life that must meet similar circumstances. In her seventh showing, she says, *"Our failing is dreadful, our falling is shameful, our dying is sorrowful; but in all this, the sweet eye*

of pity and love never looks away from us, neither does the working of mercy cease.

For I beheld the property of mercy, and I beheld the property of grace. And these have

two ways of working in one same love. Now mercy has the property of pity, for it

belongs to the Motherhood in tender love." [xcii] Explaining her non-dual realization of

mercy and grace brings us to the idea that we can examine our condition and allow it to

be the driving force that takes us into an embracing unity. Rather than staying outer-

objectified with circumstances, she shows us how to take the measure of our dualistic

experiences into a deeper teaching about loving. Pain of failing as well can become the

teacher from within us becoming the driving force toward breaking the dualistic

paradigm of "*I and Thou*" as Martin Buber stated.

But more importantly, the way that Julian understood God ordained for her only

what the object of her love gave back to herself. Sometimes in Christian religious

practice, the many prophetic teachings are in harmony with the Holy Mother's love of

Her Creation. Divine love is the subtle form of the Holy Mother's will and Her wish to be

in harmonious union with all. As Julian acted in conformity with the innermost being of

the Divine Mother, whether in pain or bliss, she assumed the very form of Love itself. In

this discriminating profession of faith, she became the Divine Belovéd and this is the

request that all prophets bring to their followers, "*Belovéd, let us love another, for love*

is God, and whoever loves has been born of God and knows God. Whoever does not

love does not know God, because, God is love." [xciii]

When Julian followed her "Mother" Christ, it helped her model her own way of

being, or said differently, it means she modeled the form of her own being in the

123

likeness of the prophet's heart. To shape one's self into the model of a prophetic individual, using the outer structures to conform to the inner state of love itself is a process that widens possibilities within our human experiences and transforms every aspect of one's being.

Pairing

When I was doing my undergraduate studies, I had the opportunity to attend a University in Aix-en-Provence, France. Upon arriving in France, I became very ill with constant bouts of infections and pneumonia that plagued me for almost a whole year. The duress of study and constant academic exams, changes in water and diet, and a living situation where I stayed in a cell-like room in a cellar of a home during cold winter months caused me to slide deeper into depression and weakness. I felt so disengaged from my body as I was getting physically worse as the months passed and I sensed I might not be able to remain on this earth much longer.

Looking for some deep answers, I came across a photo on a streetlight in the center of town showing an Abbayé in Northern France. It seemed familiar to me for some unexplainable reason. During a vacation break, I researched more about that Abbayé and I called the Mother Superior of Abbayé Sainte Cécile in Solesme sur Sarthe to ask if I could come and stay for a six-week retreat. She confirmed my request and soon I was there in the small quarters of the Abbayé's enclosure. It was a stark room, with a Bible on a small desk, a lamp to read by, a single bed, a chair, a crucifix on the wall, one towel and washcloth. I thought, life in the Abbayé was the same today as it was in the medieval period, stark, dark, and quiet. At least my room was warm, and that was a big plus from my cellar room in Aix-en-Provence.

I had an idea of the convent's protocol but I did not know exactly how activities ran their course until the next morning, when I was awakened at 4:30 a.m. I washed and dressed quickly, covered myself in a warm shawl, as it was very cold in the stone building, and followed the smell of frankincense and myrrh as I walked through dimly lit hallways to the main chapel for prayers. Even in this simple moment of walking to the chapel, I remembered a familiar feeling which only later became very clear.

The nuns all gathered one by one in silence. Many knelt and did prayers on their rosary and others sat with bowed head in deep internal contemplation. Out of this magical silence, the nuns began to sing in the most exquisite harmony that I have ever heard, interspersed with readings from the Biblical Scriptures. The celebration of "*Tierce*" began when the sun begins to bring warmth and beneficent charity to the earth. Their voices fell back into a silence again and then the recitation of the Prayers to the Holy Mother Mary followed. Taken completely off guard by their united prayer, I began to sense a presence enter the chapel, one of such dynamic force as to remove all concerns and agitation from my body. The mental weight of long academic hours of study had fallen from my mind and there was such sweetness in that unseen presence, I began to weep, as though releasing weeks and months of illness and stress.

Soothed in the harmonious contemplation of Holy Mother Mary's rosary prayer, I could have stayed in the chapel without any need for food. But Mère Marie-ceux, the Mother Superior came over and gently tapped my shoulder and invited me to breakfast in the guest dining area. I felt transported to the dining area and ate a simple breakfast

125

of oatmeal, fruit, wonderful freshly baked bread, and tea. After breakfast, I changed into work clothing so that I could help the nuns with their chores in the vegetable garden. Always the work was done in silence and prayerfulness. There seemed to be a joyfulness of remembrance in this large enclosed garden space, which was surrounded by high rock walls that went up to the height of 8 feet. I remembered feeling safe here and thought that now the outside world, filled with terror and war, could not harm any person. I don't know why I thought that, there was certainly no war conflagrating in the immediate area during that time, but of course I was aware of unresolved and brutal conflicts in many places of the world. There was just this familiar knowing that I had been here before and I felt I was walking again on familiar ground.

As I worked prepping the vegetable bed and began plowing the earth, I sensed how the Holy Mother teaches us in mysterious and always multi-dimensional ways, as the garden became a place of remembrance on how to nurture oneself from the majesty of earth itself securing assent into wholeness. When I followed the nuns back to the chapel for 'Sexte,' a time of prayer that marks the middle of the day when the sun is at its zenith, we began the contemplations on the Joyous Mysteries of Christ: the annunciation, the visitation, the birth of Jesus, the presentation of baby Jesus at the Temple, and then the saga when Mary and Joseph found young Jesus speaking to the Rabbis at the Temple.

It was at this moment that I had a shift of consciousness that moved away from the concentration on Jesus to that of Mother Mary. It was not until later in the day, after lunch and some rest, in the chapel when the nuns were preparing for the "None" hymns when the sun inclines below the horizon, that I perceived the Holy Mother as the

126

Christéd One. It was the reverse of what Julian of Norwich expressed in seeing Christ as Mother, I saw Mary as the first Christ and the victory of her Christéd being was her son.

I came to understand that the Holy Mother of the World gives an appearance of humanness to us as a gift. We are rather the passing appearance of the Divine Holy Mother-Gaia that is and always will be an integral part of the essential regenerative Divine Soul that appears and disappears according to the needs of the world. The more developed the spiritual consciousness of the woman who gives birth, the more perfected is her body as She is the conduit to bring forward the capacity of the spiritual Soul. Holy Mother Mary could not be anything other than the perfected Christ herself to be able to bring a Christéd One into human form, thus expressing how the unified female and male form is within.

The perfection of the Holy Mother of the World-Gaia is traced through the Divine Will imprinted in women's DNA. Some women have a denser dimension and a weaker proximity to the oceanic Divine purpose that leads humanity from the darkness to the illuminated state. Some women awaken through pain, like Julian, who had to bypass the dualisms that arose between pain and bliss to catch a glimpse of the integral unity that changes consciousness. Holy Mother Mary was one who understood how the qualities of her being were only appearing as outer manifestations of her inner being and that was the Divine Holy Mother of the World-Gaia who was in the pure state of holiness to deliver Her son to the world.

Mother Mary's Christéd nature was accomplished here on earth so that generations of women could know a way to manifest their Divine form through their bodies if they chose to do so. If they offered "*Showings*" as Julian did, this was another

127

form of birthing that integrated the celestial and terrestrial through an inextricable marriage of pain and bliss coming through vision and writing. These are just two processes revealing how the "*hidden treasures*" of the perfected individuals present freedom to humanity from the One who formed them and brings us to soulful unity.

We are so convinced we are what we think we are, we have to pair ourselves into another consciousness to comprehend there are infinite ways to see the One beyond "otherness." This we can do when we contemplate on Julian's "*Showings*" that present a quintessential history of the spiritually evolving steps of our purpose as human beings, which go beyond gender stereotypes. In Julian's experiences, we feel we descend into the darkness and misery of our negative conditions and then we profess some belief or seek out a religious pathway into the sun again. Facing that sun, we will find waiting for us the Holy Mother of the World-Gaia with open arms, those arms that never turn away, is beckoning us to recognize Her as ourselves. She is always near and ready. This pairing with Julian was the moment in my life that healed and sustained me throughout my education in France and many years later. I have never forgotten the blessings in the descent/ascent of this awareness, and I bow so gratefully to those nuns and Mère Marie-ceux who, through their dedicated lives, and who have acted as midwives for these moments of insight.

Hidden in the secret of some Christian monastic traditions, the contemplative who treasures silence can find the calm and peaceful moments where they can detach from the dogma of the outer dominant paradigm and see within Jesus as Mother and Mother as Christ and find healing and refreshment in the arms that are infinitely open and wide from dualism. This, in essence, is the spiritual sweetness that Julian offered me. What arises for you, when you share yourself with this material?

Mary Baker Eddy (1821-1910) – The Wounded Healer

"Grave on her monumental pile: She won from vice, by virtue's smile,

Her dazzling crown, her sceptered throne, Affection's wreath, a happy home;

The right to worship, deep and pure, To bless the orphan, feed the poor;

Last as the cross to mourn her Lord, First at the tomb to hear his word:

To fold an angel's wings below; And hover o'er the couch of woe;

To nurse the Bethlehem babe so sweet, The right to sit at Jesus' feet;

To form the bud for bursting bloom, The hoary head with joy to crown;

In short, the right to work and pray, "To point to heaven and lead the way."
xciv

Coming into prominence at a time when women in late early 19th century American history were not considered capable of holding any office in religion, Mary Baker Eddy brought an amazing reformation of spiritual consciousness by setting clear principles that integrated mind and materiality in her teachings based on Christian healing principles she later called Christian Science. Her ardent dedication to writing about her inner process created a copious body of work. She began publishing for the public around 1876. Her ideas about Christian Science began to first circulate among those she influenced in person, but later these writings spread to a greater number of people outside of the Boston area who became Christian Science practitioners. By 1902, 24,415 members were "*blossoming as the rose*" (her comment) all over the world even though critics were impugning her work. She responds with equal strength by saying, "*Whatever seems calculated to displace or discredit the ordinary systems of religious beliefs and opinions wrestling only with material observation, has always met with opposition and detraction; this ought not so to be, for a system that honors God and benefits mankind should be welcomed and sustained. While Christian Science, engaging the attention of philosopher and sage, is circling the globe—only the earnest, honest investigator sees through the mist of mortal strife this day-star, and whither it guides."*[xcv] Her vision was born from the deep contemplative study of the Christian Bible during a period in her life when she suffered from physical ailments. Her basic teaching focuses on the non-dual spiritual principles declaring that all manifestation is Divine spirit. She disapproved of the dualistic concepts proliferated by the scientific community that two forms of matter and spirit exist. She attests to the fact that matter is spirit and any understanding that does not see this principle remains in dualistic darkness.

She grew up in Bow, New Hampshire and was the sixth daughter of strict Calvinist parents. Her father, Mark Baker, was intensely firm in his theology and condemning of non-believers. Mary constantly heard her father say, "*Life is to be lived in the sight of God."* Although this phrase did not help her during her constant bouts of illness, they became relevant later in life. She had a brother named Albert with whom she developed a close relationship especially because her inner fragmentation, brought about by seeing presences in her room as a child, caused anxiety about her future and sometimes even arising thoughts about ending her life caused her to close off from others; Albert was always there to soothe her.

She began contemplating on Biblical Scriptures regularly, in which she found a constant source of inspiration. She sought to understand God and the true work of Christ as a method of relief from her human suffering and this began as her primary quest. Her deep commitment to humanity was the same commitment that Christ lived in his purpose to heal the sick, raise the dead and give succor to those that suffered. She continued to work with great effort to bring through a pathway to wholeness through the ideals established by the wise ones who, she says, understand the true work of Christ, *"The wise builders will build on the Stone at the head of the corner; and so Christian Science, the little leaven hid in three measures of meal—ethics, medicine, and religion— is rapidly fermenting, and illuminating the world with the glory of the untrammeled Truth." To live and let live, without clamor for distinction or recognition; to wait on Divine Love; to write truth first on the tablet on one's own heart—this is the sanity and perfection of living, and my human ideal.* [xcvi]

A tragedy hit when Albert died in 1841, but she moved swiftly from her home and married George Washington Glover and moved south to the Carolinas. She became pregnant and then George died before the birth of her son. She had to move back into her mother's house for help and then her mother died shortly after Mary relocated. She had to place her son George in the hands of her cousins, unable to care for him alone due to her own severe bouts of poor health. She seemed resolved to marry Daniel Patterson, a traveling dentist, in the hopes that he would help provide a home and some stability for her and her son. Patterson promised he would take care of them, but he proved to be faithless and this blow caused her health to tumble into further problems. She did not see her son for 25 years and began to enter an invalid state physically and mentally. She was isolated, with few friends around her, and still she tried to find pathways to healing and relentlessly studied. Her study of placebos, or as they were considered at that time, un-medicated pellets, helped her understand that the mind played a significant part in a person's healing.

She sought out homeopathic doctors and found the idea about lessening doses on the physical body causing a positive effect directed her attention to the power of the mind. She contemplated this thought for many years and it took her into a deeper exploration of mesmerism and hypnosis with Phineas Quimby in Portland, Maine. He helped her find some level of relief from her ailments. She owed a great deal to him, as it was his work that inspired further exploration. She seemed to explore the question about how the deeper knowledge of God can directly affect the healing of an individual. It was at this time that she turned to an in-depth reading of the Bible and began to formulate "*the science*" behind Jesus's healing method.

A vital turning point occurred and changed the impulse that drove deeper insight into the formation of her method. In Lynn, Massachusetts in 1866 she suffered a severe fall on the ice, and internal injuries occurred. This accident caused spasms and intense pain. She lay in bed almost dead and was not expected to live. Quimby had recently died in 1865 so she could not turn to him for help. She became weary of the scientific guessing found in the different schools of healing and critically examined the fundamental principles of Materia Medica and the different schools of Allopathic Medicine, Homeopathy, Hydropathy, Electricity treatments, and what she called the "*various humbug*" that did not offer permanent help.

In her isolated state she experienced Jesus's healing power wash over her. She realized how Jesus, "*He who dated time for the Christian era, as a Christian Scientist that needed no discovery to rebuke the evidence…about how the pure in heart can see God and discern the Divine Principle of divine science.*" [xcvii] Her health was completely transformed almost immediately; she was 45 years old when the overwhelming Divine presence dispelled all the darkness of invalidism and ill health. It is interesting to note that the doctor who called in to care for her, Dr. Cushing, gave her homeopathic powders, which she did not take. When she was completely healed during his second visit, he quickly took full credit for his methods. To his surprise, when she opened the drawer and showed him his powders, he looked dazed, opened the powders to makes certain they were there and inquired as to how did she heal if not with his help? [xcviii] It was at this time that she lost all faith in drugs and instead focused artfully on the Scriptures as given in the teachings of Jesus which she indicated was her only master. [xcix] "*If ye have faith as a grain of mustard seed, ye shall say unto the mountain, Remove hence to yonder place; and it shall remove; and nothing shall be impossible unto you.*" [c] Here, at this important moment she discovered the science of metaphysical healing and began laying the foundation of her book, *Science and Health*. Mary Baker Eddy indicated that the effects of faith were no miracle and nothing impossible to all who have that faith which is followed by spiritual understanding and is equal to avail itself of Jesus's promise, not to a select number, but to all who exercise it. [ci]

The persecutions about her work kept coming in droves as she prepared the foundation of Christian Science. Her preparation lasted 18 years and reflected a mighty wrestling with mortal beliefs showing that reason, the effects of drugs and other methods external to the body, was not useful. *"I learned these truths in divine Science: that all real being is in God, the divine Mind, and that Life, Truth, and Love are all powerful and ever present; that the opposite of Truth--call error, sin, sickness, disease, death--is the false testimony of false material sense, of mind in matter; that this false sense evolves, in belief, a subjective state of mortal mind which this same so called mind names matter, thereby shutting out the true sense of Spirit."[cii]* Her focus on Truth, Love and Spirit gave her the principle foundations for teaching Christian Science but she still struggled with the individual's capacity to understand.

She faced a difficult time with her students because in order to teach the Christian Science method, the students needed *"proof of the divine principle in man's being,"[ciii]* a base from their own experiment and experience. She was aware that misunderstanding, fear, and cruelty as the *"mental means employed at this date to kill the best among us, is more potent according to the calculation of mind power, than the stake or scaffold."* [civ] She was constantly aware of the superstitions surrounding negative thinking that influenced her students and always tried to argue against them. In an article appearing in the news about her accident, she responds to the contributor of the article in a typical clear manner saying, *"For years it has been sent forth in newspapers, the editors whereof knew nothing of the purpose entertained by the contributor of such articles, that I was sick, that I was dying, that I had died of*

paralysis, and Mrs. Eddy of Concord, N.H. was masquerading in my stead. Now if the

audible word sends forth such messages and the person who sends them is a mental

trafficker in mortal mind, who can say that this individual does not privately, use his

mental process to affect the very result that he says publicly, is affected? Why not?

Since he has said and believes, and such is his theory that disease and death can be

produced and is produced through mortal mind. The next thing would follow in

sequence that if the evil mind by any unseen process could kill an individual that it

published as dead—and desires the public to so conceive, and all this because of some

motive this individual has, to have it thus—he would use this secret means for effecting

those ends." [cv]

As she was taking on the challenge of oppressive forces in the press, she divorced

Patterson and began praying for those people around her such as her niece, Martha

Rand Baker, who was completely healed by her prayers. She began to write intensely on

her manuscript, *Science and Health* in which she began to formulate how Jesus taught

and demonstrated dominion over matter. The words that she repeated to her followers

was based on the declaration of Jesus," *"The Word"—the words that I speak unto you*

they are Spirit and they are Life." [cvi] She realized these words to be Truth that becomes

"flesh and dwells among us," that means it comes to flesh and restores all things.

She understood her work with students had to come primarily from their own

application and their knowledge of the higher material sense of spiritual being and

healing. Even though she knew that the ultimate prayer in silence was the most

powerful, it was the education of the process that people needed to bring about the evidentiary effects of Christian Science practice. There are thousands of authenticated cases that have been gathered. [cvii] The majority of cases referenced came from their association with Mrs. Eddy and their need for healing and others experienced healings after reading her text, *Science and Health with Key to the Scriptures* [cviii]. This book contains an effective series of testimonies giving evidence to how application of Christian Science works.

She rewrote her *Science and Health* manuscript in Lynn, Massachusetts numerous times and in 1875 she finished a solid draft. During this time she married her student, Asa Gilbert Eddy, who died in 1882 when they moved to Boston. Asa was her closest confidant. His dedicated support helped her accomplish and secure the foundational ideas for the Christian Science Church. At the time, few members came to hear about the work while she was living in Lynn and there was great dissension among her students, leaving her work in ruins. Asa's death (she felt he was a victim of hate) caused her to tumble into a deep grief. She retreated to Vermont with friends, and in six weeks she returned to Boston and began a new phase.

Between 1881 and 1889, Mary Baker Eddy opened a class at the Massachusetts Metaphysical College of Learning. She prepared her students to become the first Christian Science practitioners installing a method of prayer without touch: "*It will not be best for the practitioner to touch the patient while treating, as there seems to be a tendency in the minds of many, expected that the thought will act more freely without touch.*" She asked them to face darkness in human form but to stay ever vigilant toward good. The Metaphysical College became so big, she had to leave as she needed more time to write.

Theologians and writers like Mark Twain attacked her with caustic critiques that were published in the papers but he could not deny her popularity. He published a satirical diatribe attacking Eddy and her church entitled *Christian Science*. Twain wrote, *"We cannot peacefully agree as to her motives, therefore her character must remain crooked to some of us and straight to the others. No matter, she is interesting enough without amicable agreement. In several ways she is the most interesting woman that ever lived and the most extraordinary. The same may be said of her career, and the same may be said of its chief results...Whether she took it or invented it, was— materially—a sawdust mine when she got it, and she has turned it into a Klondike; its spiritual dock had next to no custom, if any at all: from it she has launched a world- religion which has now six hundred and sixty three churches, and she charters a new one every four days. When we do not know a person—and also when we do—we have to judge the size and nature of his achievements as compared with the achievements of others in his special line of business—there is no other way. Measured by this standard, it is thirteen hundred years since the world has produced anyone who could reach up to Mrs. Eddy's waist belt."* [cix]

Twain aimed at her and degraded her book on Christian Science, calling her *"queen of frauds and hypocrites,"* and when the publishers rejected her book, Science and Health, Twain felt exonerated that she has scared off famous publishers as well. Pressure mounting on all levels that revealed her as a career woman with a cult, she closed the class down in 1889 so that she could focus on rewriting her manuscript.

She found she could work in a more refined setting in Concord, New Hampshire, a place she called *"Pleasant View,"* surrounded by nature. Here in Pleasant View, she directed the affairs of the household and the Christian Science Church, which had grown into an enormous responsibility. There were struggles and anguish that surrounded her work, like the pressure put forward by leading literary authors, such as Twain. Her writing on Sadness, written in one of her Pleasant View renderings, offers insight into her understanding of those who were downcast and depressed. She kept helping others against this dominating aggression.

"There is a mysterious feeling that frequently passes like a cloud over the spirits—it comes to the soul in the busy bustle of life in the social circle, in the calm and silent retreat of solitude. Its power is like supreme over the weak and iron hearted; at one time, the flittering of a single thought across the mind causes it. Again a sound will come booming across the ocean of memory gloomy and solemn as the death-knell, overshadowing all the bright hopes and sunny feelings of the heart. Who can describe it, and yet who has not felt its bewildering influence? Still it is a delicious sort of sorrow, and like a cloud dimming the sunshine of the river, although causing a momentary shade of gloom, it enhances the beauty of returning brightness. " [cx]

She confesses she had days of anguish that clouded her work but business was growing and she wanted to support the Church and the practitioners as much as possible. She refused to be the center of attention and to avoid problems of personal idealization; she began to create a manual of rules for the Mother Church. There was to be no clergy, no rituals, and all men and women would be regarded as equals. No one person would lead but rather the Church would be run by committee and her Science would spread through reading rooms which opened every week worldwide. The free reading rooms were a phenomenon that assisted thousands of people.

She prepared hundreds of practitioners by inviting them to come to Pleasant View and read the Bible but not look at her as the power of healing and to instill the Christian Science consciousness and rid the practitioner of what she called "*idolatrous claims.*" She wanted Christian Science practitioners to turn to the abiding principles: that "*God is Spirit, God is All and therefore there can be no matter; the second is that matter is considered substance; the third that matter has intelligence and; the fourth that matter being so endowed produces life and death.*" [cxi] She continued to refine her major manuscript, *Science and Health,* and gave the manuscript to her assistant, Adam Dickey, to publish. At the age of 85, she also wanted to reach a broader spectrum of society and created the *Christian Science Monitor* so that issues of the world could be understood from a fair-based perspective.

She was not a feminist but she single-handedly opened the way for complete fairness and equality in function for all women during a time when women did not have the vote in America and First Wave Feminism was on the wing. In a letter to a writer for the *Boston Herald*, she regards gender in more equal terms. Referencing the Interpretation of the Revelation, she speaks to St. John's prophetic dream of a "*woman clothed with the sun and the moon under her feet.*" Mary Baker Eddy indicated that it did not prefigure any specialty or individuality. His vision, she says, "*Foretold a type and the type of the woman spoken of in the 12th Chapter of Revelation is chimerical, it has no more validity than to fancy a statue of Liberty represented by a woman resembling some individual form or face, than name it that individual.*" [cxii] She was well aware that seminaries and colleges were closed to women and none could enter the medical profession and these facts led her to support women in all levels of representation of Christian Science. She was not a feminist in the way we might regard feminism from a post-modern vantage point, for example, she did not take a stand against religious marginalization of women's spiritual authority, but she helped open the door to Fourth Wave Feminine Principles and equality which would come many years later in forging equal religious leadership by founding the Christian Science Church of Christ led by females and males.

She knew suffering all her life and concluded, *"All matter of things could be overcome by God who was All Good."* She understood that human beings separated the material and spiritual causing a dualistic split in their mind, and she therefore saw *"materialism"* as the obstacle. Her copious writings are dedicated to dispelling that illusion. She felt that all need to learn that life is God, that spirit should be used over physical power, the human being is eternal, and that the Divine love is infinite.

Consilience

While contemplating the set of facts that jump together in my life with Mary Baker Eddy's experiences and the challenges that affected her physical body, she brings a cohesive connection to how the circumstances around a severe accident that I suffered opened the way to a psycho-spiritual resurrection that she defined in her written work.

After working for too many long hours at the university teaching Philosophy and Religion, I came home tired and worn out. The commute from university to home was over two and a half hours in backed-up traffic. I was too exhausted to eat a dinner so I jumped into a shower and decided to go to bed. My nervous system was overly taxed and this prevented me from sleeping. Spending hours trying to fall asleep made me feel worse so I dressed and decided to go out and get some apples at the Safeway grocery store. Somehow apples always help me rest and feel better.

When I arrived at the supermarket that is open 24 hours a day, it was in the middle of the night, I headed for the apple bin through the aisle of other stocked groceries. I did not see any customers there in the store except a worker loading a shelf and one checkout clerk in the front. As I turned the corner of the metal shelving, what appeared to be a very large woman came around from the other side. She was in severe distress and began to hurtle toward me, as though she was falling out of control. I had no time to move out of the way and her heavy body thrust into mine and threw me back against the metal shelving and then onto the floor with her body on top of me as well as the merchandise on the shelves. Her weight acutely impacted me severely as I am very small in physical form. While she was on top of me, I realized she was having an epileptic seizure and needed assistance as soon as possible. I somehow managed to roll her off of me and I called for help and yelled for one of the clerks to call 911. I never found out the name of the person after the medics arrived. They transported her off to the hospital and I picked up my apples, came back home entirely shaken by the ordeal, ate my apple, did some nightly meditations to calm down, and then took another shower and went to bed.

I did finally sleep that night but when I woke up the next morning, I was completely paralyzed. Only my eyes and mouth worked. I could not move any of my limbs and could not turn my head from side to side. I was in terrible pain if I did move, and I was unsure of the consequences of the night's experiences. My husband called an ambulance and I was immediately taken to a hospital for analysis.

The spinal surgeon that examined me said that I had severe tearing of the nerves and muscles and some bones were dislodged in and round the spinal column. It would take many months before we would know the true nature of this injury. The doctor did alert my husband that he must prepare himself, if the matter became grave, and to consider the possibility of having to deal with a wife who could no longer walk or support herself. I was given pain pills and sent home after X-rays, CT scans, etc. to wait it out. As one could imagine, I was terribly swollen and black and blue all over. My state of mind was looking at the inevitable ending of everything that I thought was my active life up to this point. I was too much in shock to be frightened; I was more perplexed at the changes before me and worried about my husband who seemed far more distressed than I was.

Weeks passed and I did not recover swiftly. Every day was long and arduous, the bruising was horrible, and the pain remained intense. I lowered the dose of pain pills as they fogged my brain and I could not maintain spiritual recitation of prayers or concentrate my mind on healing my body. Somehow in the subtle matter of the body, which possesses the spiritual perception as Mary Baker Eddy indicated, our prayer can reach into time and space and connects with those spiritual beings who are trained to hear an emergency call sent out with a sincere wish. Indeed, my esteemed Raga music master who was a Chisti Sufi, Guru-ji Pandit Pranath, heard my prayer. He called by phone and told my husband he was instructed in his dream to come over to see me immediately. He arrived shortly after his call with two beautiful women students. He sat beside my bed in silence for what seemed to be an hour, looking at me and listening. He simply asked me after all that time, what prayers I was doing. I told him about my practice and he just nodded his head and went back into deep silence. Then, after another long period of silence, he stood up and came over to me, and looking at me with intense eyes, transmitted a mantra that a Yogi whom he'd met in India many years ago had given to him with the prediction that he would give this mantra to someone who would need it in the future. He asked me to recite it many thousands of times. In good faith through the love I felt coming directly from his heart to mine, I did just as he instructed and then fell into a blissful sleep. When I woke up the next morning, I actually got out of bed and stood up for the first time in months. I was wobbly but I stood up.

How deeply these meditations and mantras, filled with the light of the compassionate Creator, that transmutes things of physical substance into a physiology of resurrection, changed my being once again as it did in the Abbayé in France. The gift of healing and alchemy was transported through the blessing of a mantra from a Yogi somewhere in India, to Guru-ji, to me. The spiritual beings living in this earth's third dimensional reality can occupy the sum healing alchemy of that which lives in the fifth dimensional reality of spirit. Mary Baker Eddy said "matter is spirit" and I attest there is truth to this. There is support between both realms of reality because of the current that flows through the vibration of body, breath, soul and intelligence. Psychically the Divine powers of a loving consciousness brought balance and resolve to my distress.

In consilience with Mary Baker Eddy, when she lay in bed after her fall on the ice in Lynn, Massachusetts, against the odds of her doctor's analysis, she invalidated the rationalistic physical argument which is on a lower level of consciousness to the living, psychic energies of love that passes the psychical realm into the realm of the soul. One can clearly sense how the essence of Mary Baker Eddy's prophetic work produces a positive and lasting psychic effect on the interiorized material components of the physical form. So in that sense, it can be said that prayer and vibrations hidden in the spiritual mantra alchemically work with the elements of the human body and transmute the elements by the subtle organ of perception. Mary Baker Eddy dispels the separation of matter and spirit and she postulates that mind and matter are one and the same spiritual energy, a constituent of what all material matter is composed as it is of the same, pure spiritual essence.

In my own experience in my bed, knowing well the limitation that could have distracted me from gaining mobility, I came to the same conclusion with Mary Baker Eddy and I activated psychic energies that radically transformed my relationship with my body and called it into alignment with my soul. This allowed me to stand up. I knew I wasn't done here with my earth plane work and I had inner development to do. As a student of the spiritual path, I had to experience this with my own heart's knowing. I could not believe or take into my mind the proclamation of the doctors who did not know me. I honored the doctor's expertise and counsel but I did not want them to deny what I knew to be true. I remained silent and continued to do the inner work that allowed me to become fully functional. It was at this time that a synthesis of matter and spirit, male and female gender, Mother Creator and Father Creator came into alignment as the step to Fourth Wave Feminine Principles began to reveal itself to my consciousness. I began the outline for this book while healing my body on the way. Have you ever had an experience when you healed from some illness where everything you knew in the past disappeared and you finally brought into creation something that you always wanted to do?

Hazrat Babajan (Gul-rukh-Rose-faced) (d. 1931 in Poona). The Itinerate Sufi Dervish

"One evening when Merwan (Meher Baba) was sitting near Babajan in silence, and as he was about to depart to return home, Babajan held his face in her hand and kissed him on the forehead. Instantly Merwan lost all consciousness of 'duality' and became One with God. His 'self' merged into the real infinite and indivisible 'Self' of consciousness. The purpose of Merwan's life was revealed. [cxiii]

Hazrat Babajan was Pathan by blood but Muslim by birth. Pathans come from the harsh mountain ranges of Afghanistan. It is known historically how these tough, warrior-like mountain people have great endurance and their strength tested expansionist conquerors such as Alexander the Great, Genghis Khan, and Soviet soldiers during the invasion as late as 1979. Some say the Afghanis fled to Pakistan, which borders on the Hindu Kush (Mazar-i-Sharif) where Timurid legend says Ali, the son-in-law of the Prophet Mohammed (SAAwS), is buried.

Historically women did not hold positions of spiritual authority in Muslim communities. When authority was given to a woman it was always though her husband. In Sufi tradition male authority was also tied to Arab, Iranian, and Afghani cultures. The predominant male population always subsumed women's roles and demanded subservience to the male. Female gender restriction changed in later Sufi orders such as Sufi Movement International that arose in Europe in the early 19th century when the great Sufi mystic, Hazrat Inayat Khan, brought a synthesis of four major Sufi Orders (*Tariqas*): the Chisti, Naqshabandi, Qadiri, and Suhrawardi. He formed a unique integration of ancient principles of wisdom that advocated spiritual liberty moving away from doctrinal regulation where cultural infusion had restricted women and which had overshadowed traditional schools. He initiated women as spiritual teachers (*Murshidas*) and provided a fair and equal acknowledgment of gender for the Message of Love, Harmony, and Beauty to reach around the world.

One of the great female mystics that moved away from doctrinal religious and cultural restriction in Sufi practice was Rabia al-Adawiyya of Basra (850 AD), who reached to the ranks of Saint. Rabia's spiritual achievements rose to the forefront of history when a British scholar, Margaret Smith, investigated early Sufi communities and found that many gave the rank of Saint to women. This parity among women and men in some dervish orders from Ottoman Turkey such as the Bektashiyya offered spiritual freedom to women as it was known that women conducted mystical assemblies in their homes and proliferated esoteric teachings under the protection of the Sufi Bektashiyya. But generally, women were hindered by prejudices in spiritual functioning due to religious and cultural restrictions of the time. Even Fatimah, the Prophet Mohammed's daughter, was not mentioned in *Khutba* (prayer at the Mosque) after her husband Ali

was killed (circa 570-632 AD). *Khutbah*, the Friday prayer in Muslim practice, *"is both*

the mirror and the reflection of what is going on in the political scene."[cxiv] The evening

prayer usually mentioned the political sovereign of the time and *"it is the accurate*

barometer of subtle negotiations between the spiritual (Caliph) and the secular (the

military chieftains) who declare themselves heads of state." [cxv] This type of Shari'a law

placed many obstacles before women regarding their roles in spiritual leadership when

Gul-rukh was born.

Her father was a chieftain of Baluchistan created by Ahmed Shah where the

warriors were known for their great skill in swordsmanship. The warriors created fierce

sword dances, which became legendary because in their frenzy they would inflict

wounds upon their bodies that would heal instantaneously after the dance was

completed. It is said that Pathans considered themselves descendants from the Hebrew

race and regard Saul as their ancestor. The empire extended at the time of Gul-rukh's

youth to the Punjab, which was the southernmost geographical link between Iran and

India. The Baluchis, people from the Western Iranian group in Pakistan, were believed

to be devoted Sunni Muslims, and the Naqshabandi Sufis were popular in that area.

The Naqshabandhi Sufis were known for their discipline and deep dedication to

the ancient teachings given by their founder, Bahauddin Naqshaband of Bokara, which

started in the 14th century. Bokara was one of the largest intellectually developed Persian

cities in Uzbekistan. Bahauddin was the student of the famous Baba El-Samasi who was

credited for revivifying spiritual training back to the ancient practices passed from

Hermes of ancient Egypt. He focused on methods of inner realization born from silence and retreat (*Khilvat* - enclosure) from the world. The Naqshabandi Sufis always tried to work with the political/social framework of the culture and never exposed themselves to the existing political powers that would risk getting their gatherings shut down or worse exposing their members to threat of any kind.

Resident Sufi masters surrounded Gul-rukh and although she was brought up in Afghani aristocracy and well educated in philosophy and the sciences, she was also fluent in Persian, Arabic, and Pashto the language of Pathans. Her skillful mental powers desired higher meaning to that found in her enclosed environment, and she sought to break free from the bondage that women faced in her time.

As tradition would have it, at the age of 14 a female was married off in an arranged marriage. Before the marriage was consummated, she ran away leaving her life and the safety (*purdah*) that protected women from bandits, soldiers, and all men who would regard female independent action as worthy of severe punishment, often rape and a life of degradation. She traveled to Peshawar by walking through the Khyber Pass leading to Kabul alone and penniless. Passing through many dangers where her young life was at risk, she finally arrived at the entry Gate of Kabul and entered into what she considered a new life of freedom.

Familiar with Sufis, she somehow made her way to a Qadiri Sufi Khanqah (a Holy Sufi house of prayer) and began to work there as a servant. Abdul Qadir Gilani in Nip, the Gilan district south of the Caspian Sea, started the Qadiri order. Later his disciples spread his teachings into Kabul and areas in the Punjab. The Qadiri Sufis specialized in the induction of spiritual states (*Hadrat*), ecstatogenic dance/movement techniques combined with disciplined scholarly study. An advanced student who had studied with a

150

master Sufi, Hayat al-Mir, and who organized the Qadiri activity in the Punjab offered to allow her access into the study groups. There in the study groups, she met masterful Sufi teachers as well as a disciplined spiritual guide, Shivanarayana, a teacher who blended Hindu and Moslem principles in seamless confluence. He demanded utter observance in mental training, and after studying with him for 17 months in total solitude, her awareness shifted and her insights increased. This was a major transformative moment in Gul-rukh's development.

She gained deep knowledge (*marifah*) through the advanced condition and expansion of her sense faculties. She traveled around the Punjab meeting and interacting with the different communities that were religiously pluralistic and multi-cultural. These groups revealed a veritable melting pot of Hindu, Christian, Jewish, Sikh, and British intellectuals from the West.

Gul-rukh spent years in this rich blend of religious and cultural fusion, and at the age of 37 she traveled to Multan and met up with another Qadiri Sufi teacher, Bulla Shah (1680-1758), famous for his philosophic understanding and esoteric development. Gul-rukh had by this time spent almost 25 years in some form of Sufi discipline and now, with the influence of this great master, she entered what is termed the perfect condition of the effacement into Divine Consciousness and the stabilization of the expanded state (*Fana-Baqa*).

For years she engaged with the surrounding community improving conditions all around her but living as a mendicant dervish. At the age of 65, she arrived in Bombay around the early 1900s. It is recorded in the biographies of many great mystics such as Hazrat Inayat Khan and Beher Baba that she was a living example of a tribal woman

151

who showed great strength and endurance and gained the status *of "Mother to the Saints of the times."* [cxvi] It was because of her that these two great souls followed their destiny path after she acknowledged both their stations of Divine awareness that blessed them (*Baraka*) and led them into their spiritual work in the world. This ancient form of blessing (*Baraka*) was passed to them in the same manner that the great Sufi Master, Khawaja Gharib Nawaz Moineddin Chisti, received his blessings when the appearance of the mystic Hazrat Ibrahim Qandoozi came into his garden and offered him some oil cake from his mouth that he was chewing. The illumination was so fervent; the great Khawaja gave all his possessions away to the poor and began to travel the subcontinent in search for truth. Gul-rukh, now Hazrat Babajan, passed the same food of illumination to Hazrat Inayat Khan and Meher Baba, two men whose spiritual work have guided millions in the 20th century on the spiritual journey.

She overcame the biological profiling of women of her time who were caught in the limited sociopolitical standards that refused to recognize spiritual advancement and authority in women. She lived as a poor mendicant dervish, which was a nonviolent action to not participate in the indoctrination or domination strategies of the political climate surrounding women. As one might expect, thieves, who were fanatical religious leaders tried to imprison her alive in a grave, threatened the conditions under which she lived, and even children threw stones at her for eccentric behavior. [cxvii] Yet, withstanding all levels of threat, she was loved by many groups of people from different belief systems who regarded her as a *"Qalandar,"* a great Sufi Master who used unorthodox strategies to help all people and who was not affiliated to any Sufi Order.

When she returned in 1910 to Poona, India, where she remained for the rest of her life, she maintained the same strategy of behavior. She always dressed as a mendicant and, finding her residence under a neem tree at the entry of the village, people could visit her freely and seek her blessings (*Baraka*) and Holy glance (*Darshan*). Her spot under the neem tree was becoming popular as many heard about her skillful intuitive insight and generosity to address everyone who came to her, and people did not hesitate to travel far and wide to be in her healing spiritual presence.

There was an incident one day when people were gathered around her where she stood up and started screaming about the severe pain, tearing her hair and yelling uncontrollably; she frightened most who were sitting with her. Many thought she had gone mad, but soon a member of the adjoining community came into her midst and declared that a church was attacked by oppositional forces and all in the church died from fire. In this instance all could grasp her extended love of the community and the inner connection she had with all beings in the surrounding area.

Her popularity and resident position at the gate of the town embarrassed the British and they soon suggested she shift her meeting place to a makeshift shack away from the entrance of the village, which they were willing to provide for her. She refused their offer and sitting under the neem tree people began calling her *"The Abdal"* or transformed one. As her legend began to spread, although she gave no external practices and emphasized no affiliation to any system, she became known as *Hazrat* (Master), *Baba* (Father), *Jan* (Soul). She was heard saying to women that they must become a man, in order to break the inherent strategy of dominance over their Divine inheritance. She often referred to herself in the male form and not by the female gender, thus bringing herself into full spiritual authority and equality within the religious system that would indicate otherwise. Her urge toward balancing the imbalance was a bold and courageous act by a woman under the historic conditions of the time. For she brings forth the Holy Mother in her inherent female form as the Creator Principle and the male as the supporting principle of action on the stage of life. Saying she was male revealed the possibilities to men about how to regard a woman as an equal and to a woman how to be the Active Principle, meaning what a woman contributes through their soul freedom, therefore defines the essential step toward spiritual liberty. Her instruction to women is a fitting Fourth Wave Feminine Principle and deserves great reverence, particularly concerning the religious/political constrictions in which she lived.

The poor areas in the village improved with her presence and blessings. Many new businesses sprung up and prosperity came to the people because of her spiritual magnetism and generous healing *Baraka*. She never had any privacy and even when a thief tried to steal her shawl at night, she lifted up her body so he could take it. She saw all beings as children of the Divine and never turned against that view. When the people of the village became angry and wanted the thief arrested, she opposed the arrest. [cxviii]

All her life she regarded others in a sacred manner. She passed through the patriarchal blockages and entered spiritual authority previously limited to women before her. None could match her strength and audacity; she was free to be in full spiritual authority, not through her affiliation with any organization but in full presence with Divine awareness, always generous and loving of all beings.

A transcendental co-presence

One cold, rainy day, when I was 13 years old, I went into an esoteric bookstore called Samuel Weiser's in New York City's West Village. The store had a wonderful musty smell and one that called the mind into rooms of contemplation. As I gazed around the shelves of old manuscripts, a book suddenly fell on my head from the higher shelf. When I looked down on the floor it was a Sufi Message Volume by Hazrat Inayat Khan entitled *In an Eastern Rose Garden*. I picked up the book and opened it to the first page, which had a photograph of a man. I immediately recognized his face and fell into what I can now call a cosmic swoon. I don't know how long this experience lasted but I was certain I knew him and from that moment I was going to find out everything I could about this mystic, Hazrat Inayat Khan. Miraculously, I began to meet Sufis everywhere without really knowing who the Sufis were.

Applying co-presence and correlating the same intuitional experiences with the life of Hazrat Babajan, within a short period of time I remembered meeting the many Sufi masters such as Jerrahi Sufi Sheikh Nur al-Anwar Jerrahi, Lex Hixon, and took hands with his teacher Sheikh Muzaffer Ozak al-Jerrahi at Columbia University in New York City. Shortly after meeting Sheikh Muzaffer, I took a journey to Morocco and met a Qadiri Sufi, Sheikh Ameen, in the marketplace selling vegetables. Caring for my safety, as I was a young woman traveling alone, he invited me to his home for a meal and prayers. I found out he was a leading Qadiri Sufi Master in the area. When I journeyed later to San Francisco, I met and befriended Irina Tweedie, a female Naqshabandi Mujaddiya Sufi master. We would meet and do Zikar (Sufi Prayer) together and share insights into contemplative practices given by her master Sufi teacher, Bhai Sahib (Elder

Brother). Later in London, I studied with the Nimatullahi Sufi Master, Jerrard Nurbaksh, who was also a professor of philosophy at the Sorbonne in Paris. It was Dr. Nurbaksh's deep insight that inspired my path into an academic life. In France, I studied with the eldest son of Hazrat Inayat Khan, Pir Vilayat Khan, for a long retreat (khilvat) in the French Alps, in Chamonix, studying the alchemical process of spiritual transformation that he skillfully designed. I then worked with Inayat Khan's youngest son, Pir Hidayat Inayat Khan, who was the Pir of the Sufi Movement International in Amsterdam, Holland. Truly these were gifts of training by association. New Sufi relationships developed with Pir Moineddin Jablonski of the Sufi Islamia Ruhaniat Society (now called Sufi Ruhaniat International) and Murshid Saul-uddin Barodofsky of the Dervish Healing Order that were blessed with insight and inspiration, and my heart felt the presence of the Divine caravan of lovers that the mystical schools of Sufis always talk about in literature.

Over 50 years later, and after having studied with the different teachers of various Sufi Orders (*Tariqas*) and predominantly the Sufi schools that were transmitting the Message of Hazrat Inayat Khan's teachings of Spiritual Liberty, which have spread worldwide, I had discovered an amazing realization. Although all the methods were different, the universal message of the many Sufi orders corresponded perfectly. It seemed to me all the Sufi Schools regarded the world as a place where perceived external energies were merely the shadows of infinitely deeper internal realities. The masters of mystical vision all realized that the spiritual world of individuals (if individuals did indeed exist) were in contiguous confluence with inner spiritual unity (*Tawhid*). The archetype that existed was that essence of love flowing from the open heart that would not allow distinctions and differences to separate the male from the female, the heaven from the earth, the microcosm from the macrocosm, or the thief from the master. It was at this point in my awareness that Hazrat Babajan's true knowledge is that of the highest and deepest awareness of the infinite. She knew that human beings were ignorant of themselves as they only regarded the continual outer changes but not that which was and is eternal. She saw all happenings, such as the experience of the thief taking her shawl at night, as an external and superficial action yet she recognized it from the view of the Infinite, thus...she lifted up her body so the thief could succeed. As Sri Aurobindo says, *"This knowledge is not possible to the mind; it can only be reflected inadequately by it when it is touched by a ray from the secret luminous cavern of our superconscient being; yet of that ray we can make a shining ladder to climb into the source of this supreme self-viewing wisdom."* cxix

Hazrat Babajan was the Holy Mother of great masters that brought the Sufi Message to millions of people worldwide. She broke the barrier for women to be regarded not as an equal but superior to the cultural standard that would diminish her. Spiritual liberty is a Divine Right given to all humanity. When humanity has passed through the many stages of earthly evolution, one who arrives at the stage that Hazrat Babajan arrived at will come to understand the Divine in all.

As Hazrat Inayat Khan so clearly articulates, *"If a friend comes to meet them, to the Sufi it is God who is coming to them; if a beggar is asking for a penny, it is God whom the Sufi recognized in that form; if a wretched person is suffering misery, the Sufi sees also the existence of God. Only, the difference is that in some she/he sees God unconscious; another person sees God conscious. All those who love the Divine, who hate the Divine, who like or dislike the Divine, who look upon the Divine with admiration or contempt, the Sufi looks at with the eyes of the worshipper of God, who sees the Belovéd in all aspects."* [cxx] Hazrat Babajan gave this sacred contribution of mystical insight to the world, and her archetypal evolution is one that inspired mine. While blending transcendental co-presence, hearts can generate similar meaning in the same way the Sufis meet Lovers of the Divine on the caravan of life as a flowing river to the source. May it reverberate into time and guide all women and men to perfected balance within their polarities so that all might have the happiness of a fulfilled nature.

The transcendental co-presence that opened with Hazrat Babajan was the intuitive acknowledgement of the caravan of Sufis so beautifully arriving into my life and changing every aspect of my known existence. As the aroma of the rose uplifts the heart so too does the association with the mystical Sufis. They bring the ineffable dimension that is beyond love, knowledge and experience in which the lover will taste the truth of certainty and will be permanently changed by the encounter.

Sanapia-Comanche Eagle Doctor (1895-1968) - The Reluctant Healer

Sanapia is unique and one of the last women who carried the true Comanche Eagle Doctor transmission. Her influences, training, and profoundly rigorous accounts of how she learned are truly educational about the ancient traditional healing practices that have helped so many hundreds of people. The Comanche culture does not have much historical material to obtain insight into the Medicine Way. But due to the interviews with Sanapia by David Jones [cxxi], we receive a window into an extraordinary servant of the Holy Mother of the World. Sanapia's instructors were her grandmother, mother, and maternal uncle. She was observed from a very young girl as to whether or not she had the character and makeup to follow the rigorous path of the Eagle Medicine woman. As her father turned to more Christian and white man's influence, her mother held strictly to the ancestral Comanche transmission. Although Sanapia was at first reticent to follow in her mother's footsteps, she was brought into the training program by first identifying all the natural herbs and floral medicines that grew around the Oklahoma countryside. Her entire early life was a starting point up until menopause when her real practice began. Her mother dissuaded her from marriage so that her attention would not be taken away from the spiritual practice and strict observance of ethical rules.

During what Sanapia called the "roughing period" she did marry several times and had three children. She left her first husband and married a second time, but her favorite husband died and this experience drove her into promiscuity, gambling, alcohol, and exhibitions of bad temper. She felt that grief drove these bad behaviors yet it was the "roughing period" when she attempted to employ her doctoring skills.

She possessed an advanced understanding about the alchemy of herbs and raw plant parts. Her skills in diagnosing afflictions and offering the correct treatment were intuitively artful. With the ethical training given to her by her mother and material uncle, she would have to lead an honorable life to that of the *"Pahakut"* (Doctor) as the teachings revealed that both the Medicine and the Doctor are one. If one's behavior brings disrespect to oneself, it disrespects the Medicine and this will only cause death and suffering of the Eagle Doctor and with everything else that she attempts to do. It was decided that Sanapia enter a commitment of serious training.

Finally, after her final test, which consisted of a vision quest in solitary meditation, she fought with the ghosts that attempted to harass her so she would give up the Medicine. She entered what can be called a mystical combat and fought her fears to

160

stand in the true light of her healing work. Only later did the apparition of the Eagle come to empower her spirit as a Doctor.

As Sanapia's reputation grew and more people both Indigenous peoples and White people (mostly soldiers) were turning to her for help and assistance with their illnesses, she understood that she could never be biased against those in need nor ever brag about her abilities. She discouraged others from speaking about her with either praise or blame. She felt that any speaking out about her personality in any way, positive or negative, disrupts the Medicine that has been gifted to the people from the Eagle Spirit.

Whenever she was paid for her treatments, she would accept any form of exchange. Furthermore, Sanapia knew that a portion of any payment had to be given immediately back into the community as a "give away." This was the manner in which the Eagle Doctor honored the Medicine. Never, under any circumstance, can Medicine be used for evil or for the aggrandizement of the individual. The actions that supported the community on all levels were the ever-increasing motivation of the *Pahakut*. This contribution was considered a great blessing and a spiritual responsibility that required vigilance when tests were before her, either on the inner planes through vision or on the outer reality through the temptation toward destructive self-behaviors. To be in connection with the higher spiritual consciousness was the root of everything worthwhile and the true force that determined an Eagle Doctor's existence.

After doctoring for many years, Sanapia had her first real dream. She considered a real dream as one which changed her behavior, as she considered other dreams as just ordinary. She remembers a figure that came to her and presented her with spiritual

161

items that sent a somatic sensation throughout her body and offered a supernatural power. She believed something was always helping her and that there was power, meaning power in the sense that her doctoring skills could actualize more fully from these "real" dreams and visions.

One of the most important experiences that changed her behavior came when she was in the middle of doctoring when she was singing her Medicine Song. She felt the eagle's wings and a brush of air that surrounded her. Everything around her disappeared and only the image of the eagle stood visible against a gray backdrop. When she saw the eagle, she trembled violently and broke out into an intense perspiration. Her heart beat rapidly increased and she almost fainted. She details that her doctoring abilities increased exponentially after these visions.

A Transcendental Co-Presence

While meditating with Sanapia's experiences as a young person and acknowledging how her honesty about herself and her "roughing period" communicated so fully to my own developmental teenage process about states of rebellion concerning discipline and the ability to face mature responsibilities, and while dealing with my immature interactions to my younger handicapped brother, an important incident in my life evoked an interesting synchronicity with her.

I was only in my early teen years when my younger brother was showing signs of great difficulty. My parents began to realize he was handicapped physically and possibly a Downsyndrome child. He could not use his hands correctly as they were claw-like, and his tongue did not function normally to form words. Any verbalization was extremely difficult and frustrating for him. He had bouts of shaking and spasms that were very exhausting and difficult on his little body. My parents were so patient and kind handling the situation as best they could, not understanding the full weight of what was going on, but in their desperation they turned to me. I was busy being a dedicated dancer in the New York City scene and I had no awareness of what was going to come my way. The reason why my parents turned to me was due to a study that I was sharing with them over dinner about Edgar Cayce's material from the Association of Research and Enlightenment that I had found in the local library. I was glued to these books and discussed these with great enthusiasm with my parents. My mother and grandmother, with whom I shared a love of herbalism and who were my first teachers in herbal medicine, asked me if I would like to go down to the Association in Virginia Beach, Virginia and see if Mr. Cayce had any material that could help my brother, as there were no computers at that time. Of course, receiving the trust of my family thrilled me as a young person.

I arrived at the A.R.E. in Virginia Beach and met a wise mentor, Mrs. Eula Allen (1899-1978), who had worked with Edgar Cayce and was in his first study classes. She was a guiding light to many young people including me. I told her my purpose for coming to the A.R.E. and she quickly proceeded to help me find all the writings that addressed mentally handicapped children, and I began taking copious notes. One of the most impressive readings had to do with a homemade battery appliance that would attach to my brother's spinal cord and brain, inducing a light electrical charge while four members of the family worked his arms and legs in rhythmic patterning exercises. My father, who understood all electrical things, helped me get the battery working and we began the process directed in Mr. Cayce's writings when I returned home.

Every day before I went to school and after I came home from my dance classes, my mother, father, aunt, or a friend and I would do the set program that Mr. Cayce suggested in his trance readings. We also administered herbs suggested by Mr. Cayce. Within a short period of time my brother's hands opened up and he could begin holding things and playing with toys. He began to make words, although incomprehensible to our ears at first, we began to recognize what he was saying. After a year his spasms stopped and he was walking and talking fairly well.

My mother found an institute in Philadelphia that did "Physical Patterning" similar to the ideas found in Mr. Cayce's readings that advanced my brother's capacity for learning, communicating, and balancing his vibratory body. He began to share fully his sweet self with the rest of the family. It was an amazingly dedicated effort that bonded my younger brother and I together and lasted until the day he passed from this earth. With the support of my mother and grandmother, I began studying herbal medicine and holistic methods and later deepened my study in a college in Canada that to this day have become the foundation of my life.

Yet, as a young person, after two devoted years, I had a "roughing period" where I broke loose from my family and wanted to get away out on my own to test my wings. I was only around my middle teens and it was natural I would make terrible mistakes but I had a city-wise sense about my choices that protected me while I drank a little too much alcohol and sought adventures into relationships. This did not last long as I knew that discipline was the only real freedom and I came back quickly to the awareness that there was much more to learn as the essence of learning about oneself means giving of oneself to the intuition that lives within. I was determined to find out about these matters as a young girl, and my brother was a precious teacher in helping me get there.

I saw this clearly in a dream when I was roaring a small boat out into the infinite ocean. I was happy to be leaving and to join the infinite void, but what called me back was the sorrowful sound of human beings on the land crying for help and healing. I saw clearly, as did Sanapia, that any abuse of the self is an abuse of the medicine, which meant an abuse of the Divine impulse. For me, the medicine was the maturing of my sincerity to be truly devoted to a new path in life that was opening. My mother, grandmother, and father were great models for this understanding, which was born through their own suffering.

The essence of Sanapia's experiences, particularly her relationship with her grandmother, mother, and maternal uncle, brought the remembrance of my brother and family back to me as I united with the essence of her story. In a transcendental sense, beginning with the things of life itself, which looks into self-giving as a pathway to happiness, transcendental co-presence brings insight and intuitional correlation. Her experience with the Eagle Spirit was an example of how an individual is summoned to a higher purpose. For it is through a vital communication that an individual is not living their life for themselves alone but a life that is made as one in the uniting consciousness for all. Even when we resist, a certain kind of training is going on for the development of the mind, heart, and soul of the individual. With the Eagle Spirit, a oneness with nature, and a direct intuitional sensing of the animated spirit of the Eagle medicine way was able to cooperate with the human life and bring a salvific condition in the life of others whom Sanapia treated. I found this experience with my brother. What comes into your heart when you read about Sanapia's struggles?

Dr. Rina Sircar (1938-2018) - The Master of Execution and Exactitude

Dr. Rina Sircar was a professor emerita at the California Institute of Integral Studies in San Francisco, California where she taught as a professor in Philosophy and Religion Department for nearly four decades, from 1974 to 2013. From 1988 to 1992, she was named the distinguished Haridas Chaudhuri professor of South Asian and Comparative Philosophy and later held the World Peace Buddhist Chair at the California Institute of Integral Studies. In addition, she received the honorary title of Vidasanachariya from Calcutta in 1982, and Dharmmaratna from Bangladesh.

Rina earned an M.A. (1957) from the University of Rangoon and a doctoral degree (1974) in Indian Philosophy from Gujarat University in India as well as a second Ph.D. (1976) in South Asian Studies from the California Institute of Asian Studies. She also received degrees in Law, Oriental Philosophy, and the Abhdhamma and Sutta Pitakas from Rangoon University in Burma (now Myanmar).

In addition to nearly five decades of teaching experience and several publications, Rina is co-founder and resident meditation teacher at the Taungpulu Kaba-Aye Monastery and its San Francisco center, and conducted retreats on mindfulness, insight, healing, and death and dying in the Theravadan Forest Tradition. Her areas of specialty are Buddhist Psychology, Pali language, healing, and chanting. Her publications include a book entitled *Psycho-Ethical Aspects of Abhidhamma* (1999).

Rina was born in Burma (now Myanmar), one of the strongholds of Theravadan Buddhism, in the delta district of Pyapon, where her family maintained rice mills. She attended Pyapon State High School, where she began her study of scriptural languages such as Pali and Magadhi. As soon as she was eligible to join Rangoon University, she joined her mother and the rest of her family in the capital city Rangoon (Yangoon). Rina continued her education completing many Pali as well as Sutta and Abhidhamma (Buddhist psychology) examinations. Her primary Abhidamma teacher was the world-renowned Very Venerable U Thittila, who had taught at Oxford for more than 20 years and worked with the President of London's Pali Text Society's Mrs. Rhys Davids and I.B. Horner on translations of canonical Pali texts. She also studied with other famous teachers such as U Posa, Dr. Kar, and Dr. Hla Bu. In addition she earned a degree in Law, specializing in equity and trusts. During her teaching career at the University of Rangoon (six years) and at the University of Mandalay (three years), Rina taught B.A. and M.A. honors classes in mathematical logic, Oriental philosophy, comparative philosophy, and advanced Buddhist Studies. She passed the highest exams in Sutta and Abhidhamma philosophy and earned certificates in Sutta-visaradha and Abhidhamma visaradha.

Rina's father was a famous dermatologist who worked with the British Army during World War II. In 1942, he was sent back to Rangoon due to a heart condition and passed away at the age of 44 when Rina was only two years old, leaving her mother a young widow in her early 30s with seven children to raise. Her mother turned to a life of meditation and began to renounce worldly concerns. She practiced her meditation day and night, rarely spoke, and embraced voluntary poverty in the midst of an affluent family. Due to her intensive practice, her very presence created a healing atmosphere and people from all over the country would come to visit her just to receive her touch. Rina, though, too young to understand her mother's spiritual progress, stayed close to her and never left her side except to go to school. Gradually, her mother taught her all the practices of healing in the forest tradition; Rina became her attendant, accompanying her everywhere, cooking for her and looking after her needs.

One of Rina's brothers, Dr. Albert Sircar, who served as a doctor in the Burmese Army, was once asked to attend a Buddhist teacher who was known as the Very Venerable Taungpulu Tawya Kaba-Aye Sayadaw, a reclusive monk who had devoted his life to the pursuit of spiritual experiences and knowledge in the forest tradition of Theravada Buddhism. He had achieved very advanced levels of practice and was venerated as a fully realized saint. Following this initial encounter, the Sircar family invited Taungpulu Sayadaw to come to Rangoon. Subsequently, the Sircar family established their home as a city-monastery for the Very Venerable Taungpulu Tawya Kabe-Aye Sayadaw.

Though Rina's mother was her first meditation instructor, she told Rina and her brother and sisters to surrender themselves at the feet of the great saint and to take training from him in all spiritual matters. Rina traveled to the Sayadaw's remote monasteries in the hamlets of Taungpulu and Tezu in order to practice meditation and to receive instruction from the great forest ascetic. Taungpulu Sayadaw's attendant monk, the Venerable Thazi Sayadaw, was also very accomplished in the fields of Sutta and Abhidhamma studies and taught Rina whenever she was in Rangoon.

The Sircar family moved to India in 1971 after the Burmese government nationalized all private businesses and educational institutions. She continued studying in India and received a doctorate in Buddhist Studies from the University of Gujarat in 1974. Earlier, in 1973, she was invited to join the Pali Text Society by I.B. Horner. She was then invited to teach in the University of London Oriental and African Studies department, but instead accepted the invitation of Dr. Haridas Chaudhuri to come to San Francisco and teach Buddhist Studies at his newly founded graduate school, the California Institute of Asian Studies (now called the California Institute of Integral Studies). After arriving in San Francisco, Rina began teaching courses in Buddhism, Meditation, and Healing, and she began to write her second Doctoral dissertation, establishing her Psycho-ethical aspects of Buddhism, thus earning her a second Ph.D. in South Asian Studies from CIIS in 1976.

In 1977, Rina took seven students to Burma to visit Taungpulu Sayadaw and invited him to visit the USA. The Sayadaw was very happy to have the opportunity to introduce the Dhamma teachings to the Western country, and even though he was 80 years old during his first visit in 1978, he happily accepted a second invitation.

In 1981, he established a forest monastery in Boulder Creek, near Santa Cruz, California during his second visit, and during his third visit in 1983, constructed a world peace pagoda. Although there were other Theravada Buddhist centers and Sri Lankan and Thai monks founded temples in previous decades, the Taungpulu Kaba-Aye (World Peace) Monastery (TKAM) was the first of its kind in the USA offering an authentic Burmese style pagoda, which housed a meditation hall. The Venerable Sayadaw passed away in 1986. [cxxii]

Rina had made a unique contribution to the fields of Buddhist Studies over the course of her long career in teaching. As a representative of an authentic ancient lineage in the Theravada Forest Tradition and as a disciple of one of the greatest Buddhist Masters of the 20th century, she is one of the earliest and first female teacher who brought the wisdom teachings and meditation practices of the oldest school of Buddhism to the West. The Theravada tradition is primarily focused on the practice of meditation, psycho-ethical training, and psycho-spiritual transformation. Rina's meditation classes and retreats in Satipatthana-vipassana were the earliest of their kind in the West in the 1970s. The Taungpulu Kaba Aye Monastery, which she co-founded, still remains the only Theravada forest monastery in the USA with the original Burmese-designed pagoda structures. Because of Rina's emphasis on healing and Buddhist psychology, she attracted numerous physicians, psychotherapists, and healers among her students, many of who attended her retreats and training classes for decades and who also contributed to the emerging holistic healing methods found in integrative medicine and Buddhist Philosophy.

Dr. Haridas Chaudhuri often called Rina "Saraswati." It was a sacred name for her as he witnessed her great skill in all four attributes that preside over the detail of organization and execution, relation to parts and effective combination of forces,

171

unfolding exactitude of results, and fulfillment. The science and craft as well as the techniques of things are Maha Saraswati's province; [cxxiii] Rina had all these qualities in her masterful being.

Rina's greatest attribute was that she held in her nature the intimate and precise knowledge, the subtlety and patience, the accuracy of the intuitive perception of consciousness and the discerning eye of the perfect worker. Her devotion to her teachers who transmitted the Dhamma to her were the guides that gave Rina the ability to become the persistent and tranquil counselor to so many human beings.

I had the great fortune of working with Dr. Rina Sircar when I was working on my Ph.D. in Religion and Philosophy. My parents always told me if you want to play a good game of chess, make sure you play with someone far better than you. Rina was extraordinary, precise, patient, masterful in all details of writing, thinking, meditating, discussing, and sharing life, and yet kind and encouraging as a mentor and teacher. Her sense of humor was free and easy and she would often catch me verbalizing the values of existence that lead to deluded thinking like worrying about oneself and one's future. She always returned my consciousness to the two main principles of meditation practice, as she was a master of meditative techniques.

The first is to learn to still the mind, to calm oneself. It is surprising but true that simply by cultivating calmness we can overcome most of our emotions and psychosomatic problems and anxiety disorders. Developing calmness through meditation is the practice, which tranquilizes and humbles the mind, making it clearer and brighter, until it is empty and radiant. In this way a new mind is uncovered, a "right-mind" which is powerfully simple, creatively silent, energetically still. [cxxiv] The second was to get beyond mental clinging to outer stimulations. This took a greater commitment and discipline.

Rina's actions in all things seemed persistent and flawless. She hardly ever slept and was indefatigable in her manner of weighing details in all actions on the stage of life and in her teaching methods. She invited me to co-teach a Ph.D. class in Buddha Dharma with her, perhaps to test out my ability in remembering the lessons that she skillfully transmitted to me and to make sure my Pali translations was up to par. Nothing was too small a detail for her attention to mold and remold my true understanding until I could successfully stand as an instrument for the Dharma itself. There was no detail that seemed superfluous. Only the admirable and complete attention to the sincere and straightforward unfolding of the Abhidhamma principles and its helpful assistance to attain every beneficial condition in life was the object of the study.

Pairing

During one of the many lengthy retreats with Rina at the Taungpulu Kaba Aye Monastery, I remembered an incident that happened while I was on another three-month retreat up in the French Alps of Chamonix, with my Sufi teacher, Pir Vilayat Inayat Khan, the eldest son of the great Sufi Master, Pir-O-Murshid Hazrat Inayat Khan. We were up in an altitude of about 14,000 to 15,000 feet and the vista was extraordinary, as one could see for miles over the vast mountain ranges and glaciers. I petitioned to stay in the High Hermitage in solitary, which was up on the higher point of the mountain for a portion of my retreat so that I could deepen my practice of meditation. It is was a small stone building with only one little window, but the vista was glorious and I was alone instead of being surrounded by other students who also came to study with Pir Vilayat.

During my practice, which became intensely focused, I began yearning to see the face of the Divine Mother of the World. Over and over, I would gaze out into the infinite spaciousness of the great mountains and call out for some answer. It was cold and the wind was terribly icy, after weeks I was becoming impatient with my plea although I kept to my formal practices assigned to one on Sufi retreat *(Khilvat)*. Exhausted with my pleading, I finally gave up all my prayers and mantras and just sat empty and free of intention and desire. I closed my eyes and soon I began to see the faces of thousands of people pass before my gaze, all genders, all races, all faiths, all manner of humankind, those I knew, those I did not know. It was just their faces, their eyes. This vision of all people kept coming like a tsunami into my consciousness for many hours and I soon became exhausted and fell into a sleep. Right before I passed out, I saw my face as the last face on this wave of consciousness, and I understood how united we are to the Divine Mother of the World-Gaia. She isn't out there somewhere, She is within us, She IS us, and we are Her.

It was this infinite consciousness that I entered again when I was with Rina on meditation retreat at the Taungpulu Kaba Aye Monastery. Although the methodology for meditation were through Buddhist practice, it brought me to the same pairing and innate knowing that I experienced in retreat *(Khilvat)* in the mountains of Chamonix, France. Methods might be different but the transformative breakthrough is the same.

Rina would say about this above experience that I shared with her: *"To get beyond the intellect, to go beyond emotions, means to practice meditation. Meditation is the development of face-to-face awareness of your own mind and body. The process of meditation is the transcending of the intellectual mind, since the intellectual mind itself becomes an object of awareness. As a result, the understanding that arises from this direct awareness is very different, fundamentally different from intellectual understanding. We might call it "intuitive understanding." It is clear, directly apparent, and independent of discursive thinking and other forms of mental clinging. And it is this understanding that can bring happiness and peace."* [cxxv]

The greater our understanding, the more patient we are with ourselves and with others. Our compassion grows and our pure understanding takes precedence over harmful and offensive thought forms that hinder our lives and bind us into relational difficulties. Understanding our intuitive nature generates compassion; this is a Buddhist awareness that hinges itself to moral conduct (*Sila*) and guides the practitioner unerringly on their way. Clinging to views that are grasping at outer reality or being controlled by outside forces in culture or dogmatic codifications that want to control and dominate, instead of that which arises from within oneself, brings us again to the ultimate teaching in Fourth Wave Feminine Principles which is the call to listen and be guided by that which comes within one's own heart. It takes great patience, practice, and discernment, which is absolutely necessary. Rina reiterated constantly how she was instructed also by the great teachings of the Buddha who offered the invitation to all to come and see for themselves, *"Ehi-passiko"* and to *"Strive on untiringly"* (Buddha's last words to his disciples).

When Rina's work was finished, it appeared that every detail was smoothly in place and nothing was left out. Rina like Goddess Saraswati, all manner of things was accurate, complete, and admirable. Nothing short of perfection satisfied her and she was ready to face an eternity of effort if that was needed for the fullness of her study and work in the world. Rina was undaunted by dominant patriarchy held so firmly in the Buddhist transmission and moved steadily toward her goals without delay or activation by self-doubt. As Sri Aurobindo indicated, *"Therefore of all of the Mother's powers, Saraswati is the most long-suffering with humanity and its thousands of imperfections. Kind, smiling, close and helpful, not easily turned away or discouraged, insistent even after repeated failure, her hand sustains our every step on condition that we are single in our will and straightforward and sincere;...a mother to our wants, a friend to our difficulties, a persistent and tranquil counselor and mentor, chasing away with her radiant smile the clouds of gloom and fretfulness and depression, reminding always of the ever-present help, pointing to the eternal sunshine, she is firm, quiet and persevering in the deep and continuous urge that drives us towards the integrality of the higher nature."*[cxxvi]

In pairing with Rina, I looked through her eyes at the world, and I saw the perfection pouring out of her formed by her dedication and commitment. All were completely safe in her presence as Rina's actions always brought benefit to the beings that had the good fortune to be touched by such a master of execution in action, freely moving in Divine works. This experience identified the Holy Mother of the World-Gaia as one did not feel separated from her as a separate entity but bound to Her by the same conscious force that her extraordinary love of action in the world exemplified.

Closing perspective

As we regard these Holy Women and the lives they have lived, we read ourselves as we journey into their formative consciousness of awakened awareness. Using the four principles of transcendental phenomenology, pairing, co-presence, and consilience, we introduce ourselves to Fourth Wave Feminism Principles, which becomes the balancing point for our next step forward as women and men in a society because it respects the freedom found in each soul.

We can no longer go on as a people hopping on one leg, thinking the male dominant paradigm will carry us into any level of illuminated consciousness. Our sacred marriage between female and male forces within ourselves is the ultimate experience that brings us into happiness and harmony we seek. One's total devotion needs to turn to the Truth of the Spirit within one's heart. One need not lose oneself to the mass of the undeveloped that subordinates and confines the sense of spiritual freedom to one's true fullness of being. For those who wish to awaken, realization of the voice from within is the sacred gift to us from the Holy Mother of the World-Gaia.

Each of these Holy Women opened a pathway for us as they mapped a possible route for unfolding one's soul plan. We do not need to feel compelled to follow their plan but in merging into their life stories, we open a pathway into our own as I have showed you through my intuitive connections. As I sensed mine, you will sense yours, it simply becomes a way of reading yourself into the story and merging into the presence of the Holy Mother's being.

These Holy Women have enriched my purpose over the many years. They have
been exemplars of possibilities, faith, courage, discipline, vision, and soulfulness; they
are the banner of Fourth Wave Feminine Principles. Mary Baker Eddy prophetically
forged her Church of Healing; Frida Waterhouse opened the door to one's soul plan;
Mother Teresa captured the conscience of nations in regard to how we treat those who
are homeless and marginalized; Noor-un-nisa Inayat Khan bravely gave her life to save
many families from the tortures of Nazism; Sanapia showed us the true ethics and
struggle of a dedicated healer; Julian of Norwich gave us a visionary illumination that
bypassed gender dominance; Hazrat Babajan showed us the courage to stand freely in
her royal and spiritual authority against the backdrop of religious oppression; and Dr.
Rina Sircar introduced us to untiring and utter perfection in action.

I mirrored my intuitional experiences as I traveled inwardly with these great
souls who gave me an opportunity to read myself as my experiences flooded forward
onto the pages. All of these Holy Women reveal the archetype of the Holy Mother of the
World-Gaia. The Mother of the World-Gaia returns again and again in endless
manifestations of womanhood; although appearing in gender disguise as in Julian's
vision as Christ as Mother, she is always the same One. Yet...powerfully, She vows, as
with Tara, to remain in female form, until all beings find acknowledgment within Her
pure understanding. When the individual woman is ready, the Holy Mother of the
World advances the feminine form into Her own unified and compassionate capacities.
This is the same for the male gender who willingly take on this ultimate transformation
honoring their feminine counterpart as equal. She appears courageously within every
generation, absorbing the horrors of ignorance that demeans who She truly is. Within

Her powers of grace and fortitude, She insists on acting solely under the conditions of Love, Light, and Truth. She lays down the pathway for all to return in the One Form that will remain the head of the spiritually human community and victoriously remove all burdens of limitation between the sexes. When intense ignorance, hatred, and violence try to destroy Her, She remains steadfast in Her determination to reveal the spirit of assembled armies of Great Guardians, and Goddesses. Gods, Avatars, and Angels from all realms She calls them forth in familial connection as She has birthed them all through her patience and fortitude. In Her many forms, She holds the patriarchy in her heart so that they might learn the inner codes of generosity, kindness, respect, and wisdom so that they too become faithful servants of the Divine Feminine in all beings and created things. Invite the Holy Mother of the World-Gaia to be your Guide. Fourth Wave Feminine Principles will support your efforts and you will succeed beautifully.

A Love Letter

To you my Precious One,

You came into this world to bring everything you are into the Light. What you are could not stay hidden because the Love that I gave you was supposed to pour into the world. Everyone is waiting for the recognition that comes when they are seen for who they are...their beauty, their special presence, and their unique gift of self. You are the emanation of myself and it is through my trust in you that you can walk forward meeting all the tests that come your way with strength and courage. You are a part of me and I am a part of you.

I created life and that miracle of existence is living in your soul. Your life is a testament to my success. You did not come into this world by accident nor were there any mistakes made about your embodiment. Everything is set up to produce the best working condition for your evolution in the earth plane. You cannot fail, as there are only lessons to be learned. Once you have learned the lessons that come your way, you progress to other lessons that refine you further until you are able to step out on a new plateau of being where you never separate from me.

My central cause is to take all humanity to a new level of remembrance, the Infinite, respect for everything that has life, and the embrace of the human heart. Your purpose here on earth is a work in progress. You are not stationary, you never will be.

When your ability to love is clear sighted in your being, you will take a sure step above all obstacles. You will not hesitate to regard every moment, every breath as Divine. You will know with exactitude what is relative to your own bodily truth, your intuition, and your actions. My presence in your heart will infuse your consciousness with the hidden laws of truth, life, justice, and a pervading calmness.

I hold a Sweet Reign over the whole world and every consciousness shall be illuminated by my sincere and abiding blessings whether in the present moment or in the moments that follow. Go forward into who you will become. I am with you always even to the end of time.

Be held in the immensity of the eternal becoming,

Your loving Mother

References

Ahmad, Sheikh Jiwan. (Mulla Jiwan al-Gadiri-AH 1130). *Nuru'l-Anwar (The Light of Inspiration)*. Karachi, Pakistan:Maktaah al Bushra Publications.

Alfassa, Mother Mirra. (1932). *The Mother-Prayers and Meditations*. Pondicherrry, India: Sri Aurobindo Ashram Trust, Publications Department.

Al-Gazzali, Hamid Abu. (1998). *The Niche of Lights. (Mishkat al-Anwar)*. (Translated and Annotated by David Buchman). Provo, Utah: Brigham Young University Press.

Aristotle. (2005). *Nicomachean Ethics with an Introduction by Kye-Kyung Kim*. New York: Barnes and Noble Books

Aurobindo, Sri. (1971, 1981, 1988). *The Upanishads*. Pondicherry, India: Sri Aurobindo Ashram Publications Department.

------------------(1928, 1996). *The Mother*. Pondicherry, India: Sri Aurobindo Ashram Publications Department.

Bacon, Roger. (1928). *Opus Magus, Part IV of Roger Bacon. Vol. 2*. (Trans. Robert Belle Burke.) Philadelphia, Pennsylvania: University of Pennsylvania Press.

Baier, Annette. (1994, 1995). *Moral Prejudices (Essays on Ethics)*. Cambridge, Massachusetts: Harvard University Press.

Baker Eddy, Mary. (1918, 1922, 1929, 1934, 2008*). Science, Health with Key to the Scriptures*. Boston, Massachusetts: Christian Science Publishing Society.

--------------(1998, 2009) *Mary Baker Eddy-Christian Healer*. Boston, MA.: Christian Science Publishing Society

--------------(1925, 1952, 2011). *Poem: Women's Rights. Prose Works*. Boston, Massachusetts: Christian Science Board of Directors, Office of the Publishers Agents.

Bergson, H. (1946). *The creative mind: An introduction to metaphysics*. New York:

Kensington.

Braud, W., & Anderson, R. (1998). *Transpersonal research methods for the social sciences: Honoring human experience*. Thousand Oaks, CA: Sage.

Broom & Selznick. (1963*). Sociology (3ʳᵈ Ed)*. New York: Harper & Row.

Cache von Fettweis, Y. and Robert Townsend Warneck. (1998, 2009). *Mary Baker Eddy: Christian Healer, Amplified Edition*. Boston, Massachusetts: Christian Science Publishing Society.

Central Chancery of the Orders of Knighthood. (1949, April 5). *The London Gazette*, 38578[Suppl.], 1703. Retrieved from http://www.london-gazette.co.uk/issues/38578/ supplements/1703

Clucas, J. G. (1988). *Mother Teresa*. New York: Chelsea House.

Cooper, Austin. O.M.I. (1986). *Julian of Norwich: Reflections on Selected Texts*. Mystic, Connecticut: Twenty Third Publications.

Coser, Lewis. A. (1956). *The Functions of Social Conflict*. New York: The Free Press.

Creswell, John. C. (2003). *Research Design, Qualitative, Quantitative and Mixed Methods Approaches*. (Second Edition). Thousand Oaks, London, New Delhi: Sage Publications.

Daly, M. (0000) *The Church of the Second Sex*. (retrieved 4/4/11, http://atheism.about.com/od/theology/a/lib_feminist.htm

Falk, Nancy Auer and Rita M. Gross. (2001) *Unspoken Worlds-Women's Religious Lives* (Third Edition). Stamford, Connecticut: International Division Thomson Learning Academic Resource Center.

Franzmann, Majella. (2000). *Women and Religion*. Oxford, England: Oxford University Press.

Farber, M. (1943). *The foundation of phenomenology*. Albany, NY: SUNY Press.

Freud, S. (2009). *On creativity & The Unconscious: The psychology of art, literature, love & religion*. New York: Harper Perennial Modern Thought. (Original work published 1925)

Foster, Morris W. (1991). *Being Comanche*. Phoenix, Arizona: University of Arizona Press.

Gadamer, H. G. (1976). *Philosophical Hermeneutics*. Berkeley: University of California Press.

Gebser, J. (1949, 1953, 1985, 1991). *The ever-present origin.* Athens: Ohio University

   Press.

Gill, Gillian. (1998). *Mary Baker Eddy.* Cambridge, MA: Perseus Books-A Merloyd
   Lawrence Book.

Giorgi, A. (Ed.). (1979, 1985). *Phenomenology & Psychological Research.* Pittsburgh,
   PA: Duquesne University Press.

Crowley, Karlyn. (2011). *Feminine's New Age.* Albany, New York: Suny Press.

Husserl, E. (1931). *General Introduction to Pure Phenomenology.* (Trans. By W.R. B.
   Gibson). New York: Macmillan.

Husserl, E. (1977). *Cartesian meditations: An introduction to metaphysics.* (D. Cairns,
   Trans.). The Hague, Netherlands: Marinus Nijhoff.

James, W. (1890, 1918, 1923). *Principles of psychology, (2 Vols.)* New York: Henry Holt.

James, W. (1892, 1985, 2002). *Psychology (briefer course).* Notre Dame, IN: University
   of Notre Dame Press.

James, W. (1905). *The varieties of religious experience: A study in human nature.* New
   York: Longmans, Greens.

James, W. (1960). *Letters of Sigmund Freud.* (E. L. Freud, Ed.). New York: Basic Books.

James, W. (1980). *A way of being.* Boston: Houghton Mifflin

Jentzen, Grace. (1994). *Julian of Norwich: Mystic and Theologian.* London: The

   Cromwell Press.

Jones, David, E. (1972, 1984). *Sanapia, Comanche Medicine Woman.* Long Grove,
   Illinois: Waveland Press, Inc.

Khan, Hazrat Inayat. (1964). *The Sufi Message of Hazrat Inayat Khan. Vol. XI,
   Philosophy, Psychology and Mysticism, Aphorisms.* London: International
   Headquarters of the Sufi Movement by Barrie and Jenkins.

-----------------------(1962, 1973, 1979). *The Sufi Message of Hazrat Inayat Khan-
   Spiritual Liberty, Metaphysics.* Geneva, Holland: SerVire, International
   Headquarters of the Sufi Movement.

Khan, Noor Inayat. (1939). *Jataka Tales*. The Hague, Holland: East-West Publications, Fonds B.V.

Kavanaugh, Thomas W. (1999). *The Comanches: A History*. Lincoln, Nebraska: University of Nebraska Press.

Lamsa, George, M. (1933, 1939, 1957, 1967, 1968). *Holy Bible from the Ancient Eastern Text*. (Translation from the Aramaic of the Peshitta). New York: Harper Collins Publishers.

Lebouvie-Vief, G. (1990). *Wisdom as Integrated Thought. Historical and Developmental Perspectives. Wisdom: Its Nature, Origins and Development*. (Ed. By Robert J. Sternberg). Melbourne, Australia: Cambridge University Press.

Livingstone, Dinah (Tr.) (1993). Our Cry for Life: Feminist Theology from Latin America. Maryknoll, New York: Orbis Books.

Lugones, M. C., & Selman, E. V. (1990). Have we got a theory for you: Feminist theory, cultural imperialism and demand for "the women's voice"? In A. Y. al-Hibri & M. A. Simons (Eds.), *In hypathia reborn: Essays in feminist philosophy* (pp. 18-33). Bloomington: Indiana University Press.

Lozoff, Bo. (1985). *We are all doing time*. Durham, North Carolina: Human Kindness Foundation.

Maquire, P. (1987). *Doing participatory research: A feminist approach*. Boston, Massachusetts: University of Massachusetts.

Maslow, A. H. (1966). *The Psychology of Science*. New York: Harper & Row.

-----------------(1970). Motivation and Personality (2nd Ed.). New York: Harper & Row.

Merleau Ponty, M. (1962). *Phenomenology of Perception* (C. Smith, Trans.). Boston: Routledge & Kegan Paul.

Mernissi, Fatima. (1993). *The Forgotten Queens of Islam*. Minneapolis, Minnesota: University of Minnesota Press.

Moustakas, C. (1990). *Heuristic research: Designs, Methodology, & Applications*. Newbury Park, CA: Sage.

Moustakas, C. (1994). *Phenomenological research methods*. Thousand Oaks, CA: Sage.

Neisser, U. (1967). *Cognitive psychology*. New York: Appleton-Century-Crofts.

Piaget, J. (1932). *Moral judgment of the child*. London: Kegan Paul, Trench, Trubner.

Pickthall, Mohammed Marmaduke. (1953, 1954,1955). *The Meaning of the Glorious Koran*. New York: Mentor Books-New American Library of World Literature.

Pike, K.L. (1967). *Language in Relation to Unified Theory of Structure of Human Behavior*. (2nd Ed.), The Hague, Netherlands: Mouton.

Qur'an, The Holy. (1999). Seventh Edition. England: Murtaza Bandali/ALIF International and Tahrike Tarsile Qur'an Canada.

Reinharz, S. (1992). *Feminist methods in social research*. New York: Oxford University

Press.

Rogers, C. (1959, 1974). *Carl Rogers on personal power: Inner strength & its revolutionary impact*. New York: Harper & Row.

Safra, J.E. and Elan Yeshua (2003). *Encylopaedia Britannica, Vol.15*, Macropaedia. London: Encyclopaedia Britannica, Inc.

Schmidt, K.O. (1975). *Tao Te Ching-Lao Tze's Book of Life*. Lakemont, Georgia: CSA

Press.

Schmitt, R. (1968). *Husserl's transcendental phenomenology reduction*. In J. J. Kockelmans (Ed.), *Phenomenology*. Garden City, New York: Doubleday.

Shah, Indries. (1980). *The Four Sufi Classics-Introduction*. London: The Octagon Press.

Sharn, L. (1997). Mother Teresa dies at 87. *USA Today*. Retrieved from http://www.usatoday .com/news/mothert/mother01.htm

Shepard, Kevin. (1985). *The Sufi Matriarch: Hazrat Babajan*. Cambridge: Anthropographia Publications.

Shultz, A. (1967). *The Phenomenology of the Social World*. (G. Walsh & F. Lehnert, Trans.). Evanston, IL: Northwestern University Press.

Sircar, Rina. (1999). *The Psycho-Ethical Aspects of Abhidhamma*. Oxford, England: University Press of America, Inc.

Skinner, John. (1996). *Revelations of Love-Julian of Norwich*. (Ed. and Trans. by John Skinner). New York: Image Books-Doubleday.

Sprink, K. (1997). *Mother Teresa: A complete authorized biography*. New York: Harper

Collins.

Stevenson, W. (1976). *A Man Called Intrepid: The secret war*. New York: Ballantine

    Books.

Wallace, Ernest and E. Adamon Hoebel. (1952). *The Comanches: Lords of the South Plains*. Norman, Oklahoma: University of Oklahoma Press.

Waterhouse, F. (1974). *Why Me?* San Francisco: Rainbow Bridge.

----------------(1978) *Tomorrow Never Comes*. San Francisco, California. Private

    publishing.

----------------(1977) *Life, Death Motifs*. *"Who, Me?"* San Francisco, California. Private

    publishing.

Weil, Simone (1947, 1999). *Gravity and Grace*. New York, London: Routledge

    Publishers.

Weston, M. (1988). Can Academic Research Be Truly Feminist? In D. Currie (Ed.), *From the margins to the centre: Selected essays in women's studies research* (pp. 142-150). Saskatoon, Canada: The Women's Studies Research Unit, University of Saskatchewan.

Whewell, W. (1840). *Philosophy of the inductive sciences*. London: John W. Parker,

    West Strand.

Wright, Muriel. (1991). *Being Comanche*. Phoenix, Arizona: University of Arizona Press

End Notes

[i] Gadamer (1976). Translation and edited by David E. Linge, p. 21. Philosophical Hermeneutics by Hans Georg Gadamer

[ii] Ast, Frederick (1808). P. 78. Grundlinien der Frammatick, Hermeneutik und Kritik, Landshut : Jos. Thomann, Bruchdruker und Brckhandler

[iii] Gadamer, (1976). P. 21

[iv] Spink, Kathryn (1997). A Complete Authorized Biography, New York : Harper Collins

[v] Graff, Clucas, Joan. (1988). Mother Teresa. New York : Chelsea House

[vi] Ibid., p. 24

[vii] Sharn, L. (1997). Mother Teresa dies at 87. USA Today. Retrieved from http://www.usatoday.com/news/mothert/mother01.htm

[viii] Graff Clucas, (1988). P. 35

[ix] Ibid., P. 39

[x] Spink, K. (1997).

[xi] Ibid., (1997). P. 37

[xii] Lozoff, Bo. (1985). We are all doing time. Durham, North Caroline : Human Kindness Foundation.

[xiii] Holy Bible : New Living Tradition 0002 Edition. (1996, 2004, 2015). Tyndal House Pubishers. ACT Conference of Catholic Bishops India Commission. Bangaluru, India

[xiv] Gadamer, P 26

[xv] Letters, Archives of the Sufi Movement International, Banstraat, Den Haag, Holland

[xvi] Stevenson, W. (1976). A Man Called Intrepid-The Secret War. New York : Ballantine Books

[xvii] Inayat Khan, Hidayat. (September 6, 2007). Personal communication regarding his sister.

[xviii] Overton, Fuller, Jean. (1971). Items extracted from Noor-un-nisa Inayat Khan (Madeleine). Rotterdam, Holland : East-West Publications fonds. N.V.

[xix] Husserl, Edmond. (1931). P. 257. General Introduction to Pure Phenomenology. (Translated by W.R.B. Gibson). New York : Macmillan

[xx] Inayat Khan, Noor. (1939). Jataka Tales. Holland : The Hague : East-West Publications Fonds B.V. Pages 105-107.

[xxi] Waterhouse, Frida (1974). Why Me. San Francisco, California : Rainbow Bridge

[xxii] The following sections are extracted from Frida Waterhouse's book, *Why Me*. Copyright given exclusively to Ana Perez Chisti in 1989.

[xxiii] Ibid., P. 9

[xxiv] Ibid., pages 9-10

[xxv] Ibid., P. 9

[xxvi] Ibid., P. 11

[xxvii] Retrieved 12/1/10 http://www.independent.com.uk/news/homosexuality-linked-to-genes-ethical-dilemmas

[xxviii] Holy Bible, John 16 :12, 13

[xxix] Baier, Annette, C. (1994-1995). Moral Prejudices - Essays on Ethics. Cambridge, Massachusetts : Harvard University Press. P. 96

[xxx] Ibid., P. 232

[xxxi] Lugones & Selman, E.V. (1990). Have we got a theory for you : Feminist Theory, culture, imperialism and demand for « the women's voice ». In A.Y. al Hibri & M.A. Simons (Eds.), In hypathia reborn : Essays in feminist philosophy (pages 18-33). Bloomington : Indiana University Press. P. 21

[xxxii] Husserl, E. (1977). Cartesian Meditations : An introduction to metaphysics. (D. Cairns, Trans). The Hague, Netherlands : Marinus Nijhoff. P. 109

[xxxiii] Weil, Simone (1947, 1999). Gravity and Grace. New York, London : Routledge Publishers.

[xxxiv] Neisser, Ulrich (1967). Cognitive Psychology. New York : Appleton-Century-Crofts. P. 3

[xxxv] Gebser, Jean (1949, 1953, 1985, 1991). The Ever-present origin. Athens : Ohio University Press.

[xxxvi] Farber, M. (1943). The foundation of phenomenology. Albany, New York : SUNY Press.

[xxxvii] Moustakas, C. (1994). Phenomenological research methods. Thousand Oaks, California : Sage

[xxxviii] James, W. (1892, 1985, 2002). Psychology (a briefer course). Notre Dame, IN : University of Notre Dame Press.

[xxxix] Rogers, C. (1959, 1974). Carl Rogers on personal power : Inner strength and its revolutionary impact. New York : Harper & Row

[xl] Moustakas, C. (1994). Phenomenological research methods. Thousand Oaks, California : Sage

[xli] Creswell, John W. (2003). Research Design, Qualitative, Quantitative, and Mixed Methods Approaches. Second Edition. Thousand Oaks, London, New Delhi : Sage Publicatons.

[xlii] Weil, Simone (1947, 1999). Gravity and Grace. New York & London : Routledge. (Introduction XXII by Gustave Theibon)

[xliii] Braud, W., & Anderson, R. (1998). Transpersonal research methods for the social sciences : Honoring human experience. Thousand Oaks, California : Sage

[xliv] Whewell, W. (1840). Philosophy of inductive sciences. London : John W. Parker, West Strand.

[xlv] Person communication with Dr. William Braud, Professor Emeritus, August 2008.

[xlvi] Weil, Simone (1947, 1999) Gravity and Grace, New York & London : Routledge. P. 4

[xlvii] Giorgi, A. (1979, 1985) Phenomenology & Psychological Research. Pittsburg, PA : Duquesne University Press. Pages 442-444

[xlviii] Maslow, A. (1966). The Psychology of Science. New York : Harper & Row. P. 308

[xlix] Shultz, A. (1967). The Phenomenology of the Sacred World. (G. Walsh & F. Lehnert, Trans.). Evanston, IL : Northwestern University Press. P. 106.

[l] Maguire, P. (1987). Doing Participatory Research : A Feminist Approach. Boston, Massachusettes : University of Massachusettes. P. 39.

[li] Pike, K.L. (1967). Language in Relation to Unified Theory of Structure of Human Behavior (2nd Ed.), The Hague, Netherlands : Mouton

[liii] Schmitt, R. (1968). Hussel's transcendental phenomenology reduction. In J.J. Kockelmans (Ed.), Phenomenology. Garden City, New York : Doubleday. P. 61

[liii] Aristotle. (2005). Nicomachean Ethics with an Introduction by Hye-Kyung Kim. New York : Barnes & Noble Books. P. 129

[liv] Bergson, H. (1946). The Creative Mind : An Introduction to Metaphysics. New York : Kensington.

[lv] Moustakas, C. (1994). Phenomenological Research Methods. Thousand Oaks, California : Sage. P. 37.

[lvi] James, W. (1892, 1985, 2002). Psychology (briefer course). Notre Dame, IN : University of Notre Dame Press. P. 48.

[lvii] The Mother, (1932, 1948, 1979, 2003). Prayers and Meditations. Pondicherry, India : Sri Aurobindo Ashram Trust, Publications Department. P. 237.

[lviii] Colledge, E. & Walsh J.A. (1978). Book of Showings to the Anchoress Julian of Norwich. Toronto, Canada : Pontifical Institute of Medieval Studies. Pages 59-60.

[lix] Bacon, Roger. (1928). Opus Magus, Part IV of Roger Bacon. Vol 3. (trans. Robert Belle Burke). Philadelphia, Pennsylvania : University of Pennsylvania Press.

[lx] Baker, Eddy, M. (2008). Science, Health with Key to the Scriptures. Boston, Massachusetts : Christian Science Publishing Society. P. 114.

[lxi] Sircar, R. (1999). The Psycho Ethical Aspects of Abhidhamma. Oxford, England : University Press of America, Inc. P. 122.

[lxii] Jones, D. (1972, 1984). Sanapia, Comanche Medicine Woman. Long Grove, Illinois : Waveland Press, Inc. Pages 22, 23.

[lxiii] Husserl, E. (1977). Cartesian Meditations : An Introduction to Metaphysics. (D. Cairns, Trans.) The Hague, Netherlands : Marinus Nijhoff. P. 44

[lxiv] Shepard, Kevin. (1985). A Sufi Matriarch : Hazrat Babajan. Cambridge, London : Anthropographia Publications.

[lxv] Cache von Fettweis, Y., & Robert Townsend Warneck. (19198, 2009). Mary Baker Eddy : Christian Science Healer, Amplified Edition. Boston, Massachusetts : Christian Science Publishing Society.

[lxvi] Retrieved 6/16/10. Witcomb, Christopher. http://witcombe.sbc.edu/davincicode/original-sin. html

[lxvii] Lebouvie-Vief, G. (1990). Wisdom as Integrated Thought: Historical and Developmental Perspectives. Wisdom : Its Nature, Origins and Development. (Ed. Robert J. Sternberg). Melbourn, Australia : Cambridge University Press.

[lxviii] Safram J.E., & Elan Yeshua. (2003). Encylopaedia Britannica, Vol. 15-Macropaedia. London : Encyclopaedia Britannica, Inc. P. 438.

[lxix] Extracted from the New Encyclopedia Britannica, Vol. 16, Chicago, Illinois : Encyclopaedia Britannica, Inc. P. 333.

[lxx] Holy Qur'an, 2 :187

[lxxi] Ibid. 4 :19

[lxxii] Ahmad, Sheikh Jiwan (Ah 1130). Nuru'l-Anwar. Karachi, Pakistan : Maktabah al Bushra Publications.

[lxxiii] Shepard, K. (1985). A Sufi Matriarch : Hazrat Babajan. Cambridge : Anthropographia Publications. P. 22

[lxxiv] Mernissi, Fatima. (1993). The Forgotten Queens of Islam. Minneapolis, Minnesota: University of Minnesota Press. P. 26.

[lxxv] Ibid. P. 26

[lxxvi] Rushd, Ibn. Bidaya al-mujfahid wa nihaya al muqtasis. Beirut : Dar-al Fakr, n.d.) Vol 1, P. 105. (Ibn Rushd died in year 595 of the Hejira). This passage gives evidence to the length of time the disempowerment of women has been in the Islamic historic religious documents.

[lxxvii] Daly, M. (0000). The Church of the Second Sex. (Retrieved 4/4/11, http://athiesm.about.com/od/theology/a/lib_feminist.htm

[lxxviii] Coser, Lewis, A. (1936) The Functions of Social Conflict.

[lxxix] Broom & Selznick. (1963). Sociology. (3rd Edition). New York : Harper & Row. P. 5

[lxxx] The following female scholars bring a potent insight into the stratification of society such as Rae Lesser Blumberg, drawing on the work of female economist, Ester Boserup in her book,

192

Stratification, Socioeconomics, and Sexual Inequality. (1978), and Janet Saltzman Chafetz in her book, Gender Equality : An Integrated Theory of Stability and Changes. (1990).

[lxxxi] Skinner, John. (1996). Revelation of Love-Julian of Norwich. (Ed. & Trans by J. Skinner) New York, London : Image Books, Doubleday. P.119

[lxxxii] Franzmann, M. (2000). Women and Religion. Oxford, England : Oxford University Press. P. 39.

[lxxxiii] Ibid. Pages 41-43.

[lxxxiv] Khan, Hazrat Inayat. (1962, 1973, 1979). The Sufi Message of Hazrat Inayat Khan-Spiritual Liberty-Metaphysics. Genveva, Holland : SerVire, International Headquarters of the Sufi Movement. P. 247.

[lxxxv] Schmidt, K.O. (1975). Tao Te Ching-Lao Tze's Book of Life. Lakemont, Georgia. CSA Press. P. 60.

[lxxxvi] Shah, Indries. (1980). The Four Sufi Classics (Introduction). London: The Octagon Press. P. 114.

[lxxxvii] Khan Hazrat Inayat (1964). The Sufi Message of Hazrat Inayat Khan, Vol. XI. Philosophy, Psychology and Mysticism, Aphorisms. London : International Headquarters of the Sufi Movement by Barrie and Jenkins. Pages 198, 199.

[lxxxviii] Maslow, A. (1970). Motivation and Personality. (2nd Ed.). New York : Harper & Row.

[lxxxix] Livingston, Dinah (tr.). (1993). Our Cry for Life : Feminist Theology from Latin America. Maryknoll, New York :Orbis Books. P. 12.

[xc] Skinner, J. (1997). Revelation of Love-Julian of Norwich. New York : Doubleday. P. 136.

[xci] Ibid. P. 143.

[xcii] Ibid. P. 95

[xciii] Holy Bible, 1 John 4 : 7-8.

[xciv] Eddy, Mary Baker. (1925, 1953, 2011). Poem : Women's Rights. Prose Works. Boston, Massachusetts : Christian Science Board of Directors, Office of the Publisher's Agent. P. 388.

[xcv] A 10145. Letter to Paster Emeratus, First Church of Christ Science. Mary Baker Eddy's letters are filed in the Christian Science Library in Boston, Massachusetts under numeric order that are

reflected in the following citations.To attain further information about these letters, please contact the Christian Science Library directly.

[xcvi] A10145. P. 2

[xcvii] A11693. Letters. Christian Science Document Archives Library

[xcviii] A10407. Letters

[xcix] Eddy, M.B. Footprints Fadeless. P. 8

[c] Matt 17 :20

[ci] A10407. P. 3

[cii] Eddy, M.B. (1918, 1922, 1929, 1935) Science and Health with Key to the Scriptures. Boston, Massachusetts : Christian Science Board of Directors. P. 108

[ciii] A10407. P. 4

[civ] A10404. P. 16

[cv] A10407. P. 17

[cvi] John 6:63

[cvii] Cashe von Fettweis, Y. & Robert Townsend Warneck. (1998, 2009). Boston, Massachusetts : The Christian Science Publishing Society.

[cviii] Eddy, Baker M. 1918, 1922, 1929, 1934). Science and Health with Key to the Scriptures. Boston, Massachusetts: Christian Science Board of Directors.

[cix] Retrieved 8/4/11. http://www.gutenberg.org/etext/3187

[cx] A09002. Pleasant View Letters. P. 4

[cxi] Eddy, Baker. M. (1925).Prose Works. Boston, Massachusetts : The First Church of Christ Science. Section : Unity of God. P. 31

[cxii] A10407 P. 14

[cxiii] Retrieved 3/20107, https://www.trustmeher.com/files/five/babjan.htm

[cxiv] Mernissi, F. (1993). The Forgotten Queens of Islam. Minneopolis : University of Minnesota Press. P. 71.

[cxv] Ibid. P. 71

[cxvi] Shepard, K. [1985]. A Sufi Matriarch : Hazrat Babajan. Cambridge : Anthropographia Publications. P. 40.

[cxvii] Ibid

[cxviii] Ibid

[cxix] Aurobindo, Sri. (1971, 1981, 1988). The Upanishads. Pondicherry, India : Sri Aurobindo Ashram Publications Department. P. 250.

[cxx] Inayat Khan, Hazrat. (1964). The Message of Hazrat Inayat Khan. Vol XI. Philosophy, Psychology, Mysticism, Aphorisms. London : International Headquarters of the Sufi Movement by Barrie & Jenkins. P. 163.

[cxxi] Jones, David, E. (1972, 1984). Sanapia, Commanche Medicine Woman. Long Grove, Illinois : Waveland Press, Inc.

[cxxii] The overview on Dr. Sircar was generously offered by Dr. Anne Teich who was Rina's dedicated student and caretaker for many years. Dr. Teich was a professor at the California Institute of Integral Studies in San Francisco, California and lived and worked directly with the great Sayadaw Taungpulu Tawya Kaba Aye of Burma (Myanmar).

[cxxiii] Aurobindo, Sri. (1928, 1996). The Mother. Pondicherry, India : Sri Aurobindo Ashram Publications Department. P. 50.

[cxxiv] Sircar, R. (1999). The Psycho-Ethical Aspects of Abhidhamma. Oxford : University Press of America. P. 122.

[cxxv] Ibid. P. 123

[cxxvi] Aurobindo, Sri. (1928, 1996). The Mother. Pondicherry, India : Sri Aurobindo Ashram Publications Department. Pages 53,54.

Dr. Perez-Chisti's publications and articles

1998, *Causation, Correlation and Liberation in the Abhidhamma*, UFI Publications, Washington, D.C.

1998, *Sufi Women-Journey to the Beloved* (contributor)) published by International Association of Sufism, San Rafael, California.

1999, *Commentary on Meister Eckhart's Notion of Emptiness*. Toward the One Magazine. Edmonton, Canada.

2001, *The Cosmic World-How we Participate in Thee, Thou and Us*. A Journal of Consciousness and Transformation Quarterly, ReVision. Vol. 23, Number 2. Transformation Quarterly, Heldref Publication, Washington, D.C.

2003, Italian International Sufi Journal. *Women's Prophetic Contributions to Sufism*. Verona, Italy. Italian International Sufi Movement Publications.

2008, Originally Blessed. (contributor) *Love of the Mother of the World*. Published by Creation Spirituality Communities. Golden, Colorado.

2010, ReVision Magazine. A Journal of Consciousness and Transformation. *A Feminist Approach to Three Holy Women's Intuitive Processes : Exploring Aspects of Transcendental Phenomenology and Hermeneutics through a Correlation with the Researcher's Experiences.* Spring Edition. San Francisco, California.

2015, *Peace with All – Akbar, the First Interfaith Mogul King*. Berkeley, California : Sufi Movement International of the USA.

2015, *Ultimate Realities – The Buddhist Abhidhamma Revealed*. Orinda, California. Sufi Universal Fraternal Institute.

(Photo by Saqi Lori Stewart)

Dr. Ana Perez-Chisti, also known as Aadya Murshida (Senior Sufi teacher) is an ordained minister and President of the Sufi Universal Fraternal Institute, based in California. (https://sufiuniversalfraternalinstitute.live). She is the head of the Religious Activity for the Sufi Movement International and conducts a training program in the study of Comparative World Religions, Sufi Esoteric Principles, Ethics, Fourth Wave Feminine Principles, Psychology, and Philosophy.

She holds Masters and Doctoral degrees in Psychology, Religion, and Philosophy and taught at the California Institute of Integral Studies; academically held posts as Vice President for the University of Creation Spirituality; Ph.D. Chair for the Global Program at the Institute of Transpersonal Psychology, (now called Sophia University); and designed an online Religious Studies program at Naropa University in Boulder, Colorado. She has lectured in many Universities worldwide and was the Director of the Prison Library Project. She was at the startup of the AIDS Hospice Program, and the Emergency Relief Fund International that distributed medical aid to countries destroyed by war.

.